◁ S0-ATT-466

The Apostles' Creed:

Do You Really Believe It?

D. Bruce Lockerbie

VICTOR BOOKS

a division of SP Publications, Inc., Wheaton, Illinois
Offices also in Fullerton, California • Whitby, Ontario, Canada • London, England

Unless otherwise noted, Scripture quotations from the Old Testament are taken from the King James Version (KJV), and Scriptures from the New Testament are taken from *The New International Version, New Testament*, © 1973 by the New York Bible Society International. Other Scripture quotations are taken from *The New English Bible* (NEB), © 1961, 1970 by the Delegates of Oxford University Press and the Syndics of Cambridge University Press.

Library of Congress Catalog Card Number
ISBN: 0-88207-748-1

VICTOR BOOKS
A division of SP Publications, Inc.
P.O. Box 1825 ● Wheaton, Illinois 60187

Contents

Acknowledgment

This book was prepared at Tyndale House Library, Cambridge, England. The author wishes to express his gratitude to the Reverend Derek Kidner, Warden of Tyndale House, for his many courtesies and encouragement.

The Apostles' Creed

I believe in God the Father Almighty, Maker of heaven and earth:

And in Jesus Christ His only Son our Lord: Who was conceived by the Holy Ghost, Born of the Virgin Mary: Suffered under Pontius Pilate, Was crucified, dead, and buried: He descended into hell; The third day He rose again from the dead: He ascended into heaven, And sitteth on the right hand of God the Father Almighty: From thence He shall come to judge the quick and the dead.

I believe in the Holy Ghost: The holy Catholic Church: The Communion of Saints: The Forgiveness of sins: The Resurrection of the body: And the Life everlasting. Amen.

Introduction

As a lay preacher, I've discovered that one of the most confusing parts of a morning worship service is the receiving of the offering. I've learned to ask, upon arriving at a church for the first time, "Do I pray before or after the ushers have taken up the collection?" This question often puzzles those who try to answer. They've become so used to the weekly order of service, they hardly notice where or when a particular act of worship occurs. If I fail to ask, I sometimes blunder, invoking God's blessing on the offering at a time out of sync with the ushers' expectations.

Nobody blames a visiting preacher for praying out of turn. But it would be an entirely different matter, if I were to stand before some evangelical congregations and say, "Let us affirm our faith together by repeating the Apostles' Creed." You see, in that case I wouldn't simply be rearranging the order of service; I'd be revolutionizing the manner of worship by introducing an element strange and—in some cases—somehow suspect.

If your religious background includes participation in church rites of worship prescribed by a prayer book or missal, then you may be surprised to find Christians who have never followed a liturgy, never memorized the Apostles' Creed, never sung the *Gloria,* never received the Bread and Wine while kneeling at an altar rail. Furthermore, you may be distressed to know that many evangelical Christians relegate liturgical worship to classifications called "formal" and "lifeless."

Characteristically, evangelical churches in North America insist on worship that is varied, spontaneous, individual. They reject as "vain repetitions" or "tradition" some of the oldest patterns of worship known to the Christian Church. Even the collective reciting of the Lord's Prayer may be rejected. Ironically, few of these same evangelical churches seem troubled by the custom of publishing an order of service, often unchanged from week to week: hymns chosen in advance, responsive reading from the hymnal, sermon title given.

Yet while some Christians persist in excluding the most ancient forms of worship from their churches, a surprising number of evangelical believers are turning to liturgical churches, to worship that stresses formal confessions, creeds, and common prayers instead of impromptu worship. And some evangelical churches are now beginning to incorporate elements of the liturgy into their worship, such as recitation of the Apostles' Creed.

Why is this happening? Why are some evangelicals abandoning life-long habits of informal worship for the formalities of liturgy? Obviously, their reasons are far too complex for easy analysis. Perhaps the enthusiastic excesses of the "Jesus People" have caused a reaction toward greater formality. Perhaps some of the more strident cries for charismatic renewal have resulted in closer examining of the Apostolic and Early Church traditions. Perhaps as North Americans travel more widely overseas and meet with Christians from older church communions, a new understanding of our historic connections in Christian unity helps to eradicate suspicion and doubt.

In any case, both evangelical and liturgical congregations are desiring to know our biblical roots, our common heritage with believers throughout the world and in all times. What constitutes our oneness as Christians?

It's possible, of course, to respond by pointing to the Person of Jesus Christ as revealed in Scripture. But while it's true we'll find what Christians believe in the Bible, such an answer may be too encompassing to be helpful. We can't digest at one swallow all the Bible teaches; our finite minds need something more manageable to grasp.

But how many of us could, if asked, express clearly and succinctly in our own words what St. Luke calls "a declaration of those things which are most surely believed among us"? (Luke 1:1) A declaration such as the Apostles' Creed fills our need for a condensation of the Gospel's essential truths.

Yet in distilling great truth into compact terms, the danger always exists that the Creed may become merely a formula. How often as a geometry student in high school I recited the Pythagorean theorem: "The square of the hypotenuse is equal to the sum of the squares of the opposite sides." To this day I have no idea what it means.

That's why merely memorizing the Apostles' Creed is of little value. It needs to be *learned*! Its claims need to be validated by Scripture and ratified by personal experience. Its propositions need to become living reality for all who wish to follow in the apostolic path of obedience, confessing with our mouths and believing with all our hearts in "God the Father Almighty . . . and in Jesus Christ His only Son our Lord."

Stony Brook, New York D. B. L.
Spring 1977

1

"I Believe . . ."

Credo is the Latin word meaning "I believe." From its root—*credere*, meaning to believe—come some of the most important words in our language.

"Will that be cash or *credit* card?" asks the salesperson.

The new college hopes to receive its *accreditation* soon.

An honest man maintains his *credibility* when his actions confirm what he says.

What is credit? a credit card? a creditor? Someone we owe for a product or service chooses to *believe* that we're responsible people who will pay what we owe at a later billing or over an extended period of time. When we sign the credit slip, we're asking the merchant to believe us.

What's accreditation? An official commission from an association of recognized schools and colleges evaluates a college and approves the faculty, facilities, and the instruction offered. This recommendation is given because the commission *believes* that the education being offered by that college meets certain standards: the professors are well qualified, the library and other facilities are adequate, the course of study is properly demanding, and so on. The commission believes that a student attending this college will receive a legitimate degree.

And credibility? In the past few years, politicians in particular have discovered that often their constituents don't *believe* what politicians say. They suffer—so the cliché of journalism has it—from a "credibility gap," an obvious gulf between what they may tell the voters and what they may do in political office.

One of the most disappointing statements anyone can make is, "I'm sorry, I just don't believe you." We all want to be believed; in fact, we need to be believed. Without credibility, we're easily reduced to the lowest possible level: imposter, phoney, fraud, charlatan, cheat, con man, liar!

The Importance of Believing

But important as it is to be believed, to live the kind of honest life that merits belief, it's even more important that *we believe* . . . in the integrity of our families, in the political system we've chosen to live by, in the value of our work, and so on.

What does it mean to believe? It means being willing to commit oneself to someone or something. When I board a Boeing 747 to fly to London, I'm making an act of belief. I'm saying that I trust in the skill and dedication of the aeronautical experts who designed the jetliner. I'm trusting the craftsmen who made the plane, the Trans World Airlines mechanics who serviced and perhaps repaired it, the pilot and crew of Flight #702 who control it. What's more, I'm not just mouthing high-sounding sentiments or philosophical abstractions about belief. I'm putting my money and my life on the line. I'm doing something that commits me to getting from here to there safely.

Merely believing in something or someone, though, isn't any guarantee that the object of belief deserves our trust. The reason I believe in TWA's Flight #702 has nothing at all to do with advertising jingles or with pretty stewardesses offering lavish service and sumptuous meals. I'm too practical for that stuff! Yes, seven hours is a long time to sit with nothing to do, nothing to eat; so I appreciate the few luxuries the airline provides—the stereo music, the feature film, the surprisingly tasty food. But other trans-Atlantic carriers also offer these comforts. What motivates me, then, to choose TWA instead of the others?

The answer is simple: I know a pilot on that flight! He flies back and forth every week in apparent safety. Two years ago, my sons took his flight across the Atlantic and back, again in safety. And I've seen him drive his car in the village where I live. I also respect his care and caution on the ground.

I believe my pilot-neighbor can get me to London safely because his past performances merit my trust. The same kind of reasoning determines why my wife prefers a specific supermarket over its nearby competitor or, perhaps, why you always buy General Motors cars.

Does my illustration make sense? I hope so. Yet when it comes to talking about religious belief and, in particular, the Christian commitment to God and His Son, the Lord Jesus Christ, some people fail to apply the same standards for belief they use in other experiences.

The Importance of Faith

Christians believe God because of who He is, what He has done in the past, and what He promises to do in the future. Because we believe God, Christians are willing to commit themselves to God through an exercise called *faith.*

Faith is belief put into action. I could spend the rest of my life telling you what a great person my neighbor Tom is—how respected he is among airline pilots—how confident I am of his skill. But unless I act on this confidence, I'm uttering nothing but empty words. Faith means getting on the jet Tom pilots and saying, "Fly me to London." Anything less than that isn't true faith.

The same is true in our dealing with God. The writer of the letter to the Hebrews said it this way: "Without faith it is impossible to please God" (Heb. 11:6). Genuine faith shows itself in action, and God won't settle for less. Many of the verbs in Hebrews 11, that great chapter on the heroes of faith, show faith in action. Look at some of them: By faith Abel *offered* . . . By faith Noah *built* an ark . . . By faith Abraham *obeyed* and *went* . . . Through faith they *conquered* kingdoms, *administered* justice, *gained* what was promised . . . *shut* the mouths of lions, *quenched* the fury of the flames, *escaped* the edge of the sword . . .

Now, as a matter of fact, I can't claim to *know* that TWA's Flight #702, New York-to-London, will arrive on time or even, as a certainty, will arrive at all. I hope it will. I believe it will, or else I'd never board it. But I can't declare in advance that I *know* anything of the kind.

The same is true of almost anything else in life. We're limited as humans. There's very little we know for sure. For that very reason, a class of people called *skeptics* exists. They claim not to believe anything they can't experience with their five senses. In other words, they accept only what they already know; they believe nothing that requires them to act on faith. Much to the astonishment and dismay of the skeptic, a Christian exercising faith in action can claim to *know*. How is this possible?

Knowing the Object of Faith

To *know* is to be related in a personal way. I can say that I know where I live because I've been there physically. I have physical, intellectual, and emotional relationships with a blue-gray frame house in the woods at the end of a dead-end street called Chub Hill Road, in Stony Brook, on Long Island, in the state of New York.

Now, you may tell me your address; you may even send me a photo of your house. But until you invite me to visit there—until I'm personally able to relate the street number and zip code to a community and the shape described by the address and photograph, I don't really *know* where you live.

Should the fact that I've never seen your house prevent me from enjoying a story you tell me about your family and something that happened there? Not if I know *you!* Knowing the shape of your house might be a small advantage, but if I know and trust you, I don't have to know your house. Believing what you tell me makes it possible for me to accept on faith what I can't otherwise confirm about your dwelling place.

Or take another example. Let's say you do invite me to your house and send a set of directions for me to follow. If I believe you, I take your instructions by faith and follow the route you've laid out to your door. When I arrive, I know by experience what I've already accepted by faith.

For the Christian, belief doesn't need to be an act of blind faith. The Christian isn't required to wear a mental blindfold and grope for something to hold onto. Each one of us has been given a mind to reason, and with that mind a means of expressing our deepest longings, the most profound urgencies of our being—what we might call "the things of the spirit." Out of this vastness within each of us comes either an acknowledgment of God's existence or else doubt and denial. But more often than not, even the honest doubter—if willing to ask honest questions—comes to believe in the reality of God.

This is the starting point because that same verse from Hebrews 11, quoted earlier, tells us: "Without faith it is impossible to please God, because anyone who comes to Him must believe that He exists and that He rewards those who earnestly seek Him" (v. 6). Only those who deny God fail to receive His reward. And what is this reward? Nothing less than confirmation and assurance that our faith is valid: He *does* exist! God is who He claims to be!

This assurance takes the personal form of a relationship with God—in prayer, in reading and study of the Bible, in worship together with other believers, in service for His sake.

It's all based on the character of God—who He is, what He's done, what He's promised in His Word to perform. "I know," said St. Paul, "whom I have believed, and am convinced that He is able to guard what I have entrusted to Him" (2 Tim. 1:12).

Knowing the person you believe in—having a personal relationship—makes all the difference!

The Importance of Confession

For the Christian, believing and knowing isn't enough. It's also necessary to speak boldly what we have experienced to be true about God, about Jesus Christ, the Holy Spirit, the Church, the present and future states of human beings—the whole body of God's truth.

Of course, nobody's able to recite the whole of Christian doctrine. Thousands of books contain theologians' attempts at giving systematic accounts of the Bible's principal teachings. We need something more concise. That's why a statement like the Apostles' Creed came into being, to fill a particular need (as we shall shortly see)—to give an outline of what Christians commonly believe.

Perhaps you're saying, "I really don't care to broadcast my beliefs. I don't like to foist them off on anyone else. I know what I believe, that's good enough for me."

Well, pardon me for being blunt, but you're on the wrong track. Confessing what we believe is our obligation. We have no option. In fact, confessing what one believes is one of the marks by which a Christian is identified. That's what the Apostle Paul told the Christians at Rome: "That if you confess with your mouth, 'Jesus is Lord,' and believe in your heart that God raised Him from the dead, you will be saved. For it is with your heart that you believe and are justified, and it is with your mouth that you confess and are saved" (Rom. 10:9-10).

Have you ever received a subpoena to appear in court and give testimony in a trial? Once the court order has been served, almost nothing can get you out of your responsibility as a citizen to answer questions in public. Furthermore, if the trial concerns the defense of a friend of yours, someone you love, wouldn't you be eager to tell what you know? Would you be ashamed to speak what you believe to be true?

We've been subpoenaed to appear before the Judge of all the Earth, as Abraham called God (Gen. 18:25). In this particular courtroom, however, we find the Judge Himself on trial. He is accused by Satan of not being able to keep His promises, of not being God Almighty before whom every creature must bow. As soon as we begin to give our witness to God's faithfulness, the accuser turns on us as well. It's then we find strength and assurance in the fact that Jesus Christ is our Advocate, our defense attorney. He is able, by the power of His resurrection, to prove our testimony true and Satan's charges false.

The History of the Creed

Where did the Apostles' Creed come from? During the Middle Ages, tradition held that just after Jesus Christ ascended and before the Church at Jerusalem was dispersed, the apostles met to affirm their unity in faith. Each of them, tradition maintained, contributed a clause. Their final statement became the Creed. An interesting story, but what are the facts?

In one form or another, creeds have existed since the time of Jesus. Perhaps the earliest recorded in the New Testament is the statement by Simon Peter at Caesarea Philippi, "You are the Christ, the Son of the living God" (Matt. 16:16). Later declarations were less spontaneous, perhaps more formal, such as those sometimes quoted in the Apostle Paul's letters. But all early Christians' expressions of belief affirmed that "Jesus Christ is

Lord." Paul states this clearly, "That at the name of Jesus every knee should bow . . . and every tongue confess that Jesus Christ is Lord, to the glory of God the Father" (Phil. 2:10-11).

Yet this simple declaration needed both refinement and expansion as the Church spread and heresies developed. The Church needed to identify for those who believed, what was, as Paul said, "according to the Scriptures" (1 Cor. 15:3). The Church needed a passport to verify genuine belief. In Latin, the word *symbolum* was used to indicate a military password, a sign of loyalty. One of the first symbols was the sign of the fish. The Greek word *ichthus*, meaning "fish," made a word game or acrostic, the Greek letters representing words for *Jesus Christ, God's Son, Saviour.* So today, some Christians who wish to give a sign of their faith attach a fish symbol to the front door of their homes or rear bumpers of their cars. It's a way of saying, "I believe that Jesus Christ is God's Son and my Saviour."

Of course, the early creeds weren't written down, which is one reason why we have so many unanswered questions about their history. A secret shared with only the most reliable believers, the Creed was carefully guarded from Roman authorities and their collaborators. Just as in totalitarian countries today where Christians must sometimes go underground to maintain their witness, so during the period of Roman persecution, Christian practices were often secretive.

In time, as it became necessary to defend doctrines under attack from heretics, additional clauses were added to the basic statement about the Trinity and Jesus Christ—such as the statement about the bodily resurrection. By the second century A.D., local churches were constructing their own three-part question as a condition for baptism: "Do you believe in God the Father? And in His Son Jesus Christ? And in the Holy Spirit?" At the end of the second century, Christians throughout the Roman Empire had devised baptismal ceremonies. *The Apostolic Tradition,* written by St. Hippolytus around A.D. 215, gives a clear description of customs regulating conduct of baptismal rites at Rome.

These included, as a test of belief, a candidate's interrogation by the bishop. In preparation, the person desiring to be baptized (who may have been kept under probation for as long as three years!) was required to learn by heart a longer version of the three-fold creed:

> Dost thou believe in God the Father Almighty? Dost thou believe in Christ Jesus, the Son of God, Who was born of the Holy Spirit and the Virgin Mary, Who was crucified in the days of Pontius Pilate, And died, And rose the third day living from the dead, And ascended to the heavens, And sat down at the right hand of the Father, and will come to judge the living and the dead? Dost thou believe in the Holy Spirit, in the Holy Church, and the resurrection of the flesh?

After each of these questions, the candidate responded, "I believe," and was baptized.

Gradually, phrase by phrase, tenet by tenet, the text we know today as the Apostles' Creed took shape. In A.D. 390, a letter written to Rome from Milan, perhaps by Ambrose, first mentions the *symbolum apostolorum,* the Apostles' Creed. A few years later, in A.D. 404, Rufinus produced the first commentary on the Apostles' Creed, essentially as we know it.

There can be little doubt, therefore, that the Apostles' Creed developed piece by piece during the third and fourth centuries and was augmented by later additions in the sixth and seventh centuries. Under the reign of Charlemagne, it became the official creed of the west in the ninth century.

How often did the early Christians recite the Apostles' Creed and other professions of belief? We don't know for certain. But Augustine, preaching to North African converts in the fifth century, told them to say it daily: "When you rise, when you go to bed, say your symbol, say it before the Lord. Call it to mind, and do not tire of repeating it."

Perhaps we could benefit from Augustine's advice. If it's true, as Peter writes, that "unto you therefore which believe He is precious" (1 Peter 2:7) then we should never weary of confessing our faith. But each time we come to repeat the Creed, we must be careful not to slur over its opening words.

Dr. Frank E. Gaebelein, Headmaster Emeritus of The Stony Brook School, suggests that a congregation listen first to the worship leader say the opening words, "I believe in God." Then all should join him in repeating the entire Creed to reaffirm these great truths. This will help put emphasis upon personal commitment, as all sincerely say: *"I believe . . ."*

2

"I Believe in God the Father Almighty, Maker of heaven and earth . . ."

Not everyone acknowledges the existence of God, although strictly speaking probably very few persons are bona fide atheists. The word *atheist* describes a "no-Godist," someone who professes that no God exists. But—with all due respect to sincere atheists—every reputed atheist is somewhat like the boy who says, "There's no such thing as ghosts!" But, whenever he passes an abandoned, ramshackle building at night, he whistles just in case! Because for ghosts not to exist, it's necessary at the very least for a consciousness of ghosts to linger in the mind. The boy's denial—not to mention his whistling—is in itself an affirmation of the very fact he seeks to deny.

So with professing atheists. They choose to disbelieve in Someone they claim doesn't exist anyway —surely a remarkable waste of intellectual energy. Wouldn't they be better off spending their time at some constructive, positive enterprise instead of shadowboxing the God they disbelieve? The whole atheistic concern is shackled by the very claim that atheism most cherishes: "If God doesn't exist, everything is permitted." Instead, the atheist finds himself enslaved by the need to prove himself an unbeliever. In denying the existence of God he finds nothing greater than himself and other selves in the universe. His greatest creed centers in "I believe in myself." What a contrast to the Christian affirmation.

God's Existence

"I believe in *God.*" The Apostles' Creed begins with this great affirmation of theism, the belief in the existence of God. The word for the Supreme Being is *theos* in Greek, *deus* in Latin, *dieu* in French, *dios* in Spanish. In English, we say *God.* In any language, the word denotes divinely supernatural qualities and attributes no human can claim. As the *Westminster Shorter Catechism* says, God is "spirit, infinite, eternal, and unchangeable, in His being, power, holiness, justice, goodness, and truth." By contrast, we human beings are mortal, finite, temporal in body, changeable in our being, powerless, depraved, unjust, evil in our desires, and false.

To believe in God is to recognize that beyond ourselves is that Being "wholly other," as some theologians say—a Being who, in spite of omnipotence, omniscience, omnipresence, and all the other attributes of power and authority, is also a God who wishes to meet us person to person and share His glory with us; a God who cares for us personally and invites us to know Him by name. When we do, He promises to provide answers to our most puzzling questions, to teach us how to imitate His divine attributes of love and faithfulness, patience and grace.

To believe in God is to be provided with the

answers to some of life's most perplexing questions: Why do we have such deep yearnings for knowledge beyond ourselves and our immediate environments? Why are we so restless in our human limitations? Why do we strive for that which satisfies our urges, only to discover how insatiable and unfulfilled we remain? Is it because somewhere deep within our conscious or unconscious self, we perceive that another dimension of being exists? Surely there must be meaning beyond ourselves. Meaning that answers life's most basic questions: Who am I? Why was I born? What is life worth? And when one utters the great opening phrase of the Apostles' Creed, he discovers the answers.

Yet there are some professing atheists whose disbelief in God is possibly more reverent and honoring than the glib, easy-going, casual claim of belief some Christians offer. "I believe *in* God," says the Apostles' Creed. That little word *in* makes a world of difference! Suppose the Creed had said, "I believe *about* God"? What would that mean?

To believe *about* someone or something means that your experience is limited to what you have read or been told or perhaps seen from afar. I believe what I've been told *about* Mount Everest— it's the highest mountain on earth—even though, when I saw the mountain from 150 miles away, Everest looked smaller than some peaks around it. Nevertheless, almanacs and encyclopedias tell me that Everest is the highest point on this planet: 29,028 feet or 8,848 meters high. So, I accept the fact; I'm willing to believe what I read about Mount Everest.

Or I might read an article on golf telling me the value of a relaxed swing rather than trying to hit the ball with all my strength. From what the article and my observation of successful golfers tell me, I can profess to believe what I know *about* the power of relaxation. But until I use the technique myself—until I commit myself to swinging my golf club without tension throughout my neck, shoulders, and the rest of my body—I can't claim to believe *in* relaxation, even though I talk about relaxation as the key to improving my golf game.

Belief *in* God means advancing beyond merely acknowledging His existence. That's a logical starting point, of course, as we've already noted in Hebrews 11:6. But what the Creed declares is a daring commitment, an abandoning of ourselves to God.

The Reverend Jack Heinsohn, pastor of Immanuel Presbyterian Church in Los Angeles, was a circus aerialist as a young man. He tells of the struggle facing every beginning trapeze artist when he first attempts the flying bar. Only when he throws himself off the platform and grabs the bar can he hope to keep from falling into the net—or worse, to the floor many feet below.

The Fatherhood of God

"I believe *in God*" means that I acknowledge who He is and on that basis commit myself wholly to Him. In the language of Jude's ecstatic doxology, our God is the One "who is able to keep you from falling and present you before His glorious presence without fault and with great joy" (Jude 24).

But while the main word for the Supreme Being we worship may be God, He has many names by which He chooses to be known. His title is *God;* His names begin with the most precious, *Father.*

So we gladly say, "I believe in God the Father," ascribing to Him all that divine fatherhood connotes.

In what respects is God our Father? As the following phrase, "Maker of heaven and earth" declares, God the Father deserves to be recognized as Creator—and we'll speak of Him as such soon. But even in passing, it's important to point out that the God we know as Father is responsible in His paternal care and concern for His creation. He is no Zeus, peopling the world with offspring of his lust, then leaving them to fend for themselves. We aren't foundlings in a cosmic orphanage.

As Father, God gives to all His created children out of the bounty of His common grace. As Jesus said in the Sermon on the Mount (Matt. 5:45), sunshine and rainfall are granted alike to Sunday churchgoers and Sunday gardeners; to the man who pays his taxes and to the cheater. Common grace is the beauty of nature, the loving affection of a pet, the provision of water when we're thirsty, heat when we're cold. Common grace is available to us through the love of other human beings, through the talents they use to promote our good.

God the Father also blesses us with common grace in another dimension. There's a lot of evil in this world. But if you think about it, you may agree that the world isn't as cruel as it might be. For all their sinfulness, people aren't quite as ornery as they're capable of being. We sometimes call it *civilized behavior*. We credit civilization with keeping wicked men from perpetrating all the wickedness of which they are capable.

But it isn't civilization that deserves the credit, because civilization itself is another evidence of

God's common grace. A handshake from an opponent who's been fairly and squarely squashing you all afternoon in a football game: we may call that *sportsmanship,* but it's really another example of common grace. The smile from a stranger, or his stopping to help you change a flat tire: that's not merely *courtesy,* it's common grace.

So too with God's power to restrain evil, to keep it under some control. We have a wonderful instance in recent history. The authorities in the Soviet Union didn't dare execute Aleksandr Solzhenitsyn, the Nobel Prize novelist and critic of their regime. Not because he was famous and his death would have called forth international protests at the outrage, but because somewhere within the conscience of godless men, God is still at work. As the Father of His creation, He restrains His fallen creatures from being as wicked as they might be.

In addition to common grace, theologians tell us about God's special grace. This attribute reveals another characteristic of God as our Father. God's special grace is His gift of salvation to all who have *especially* asked for it. Special grace is that special kind of Son-shine that Paul writes about when he says, "For God who said, 'Let light shine out of darkness,' made His light shine in our hearts to give us the light of the knowledge of the glory of God in the face of Christ" (2 Cor. 4:6).

Let me try to illustrate the difference with a personal analogy. I coach track at The Stony Brook School. Both my sons and daughter have been members of our team. When we're all together on the track, as coach and athletes, my interest is in all those boys and girls under my supervision who run or jump or throw. Their safety, their success, their pleasure in the sport, their disappointment—these are my concern and the concern of my colleagues, Marve Goldberg and Jim Adare. We sometimes become deeply enough involved to act like fathers to these teenagers. We want the very best for them; their joy becomes our joy, their pain our pain. But we realize that in sport, as in agriculture, both sun and rain are necessary to growth.

But when my sons and daughters and I are in our own home, we possess a different relationship. I'm still their coach, but far more—I'm their father! In ways that can never be transferred to any other members of my squad—and for reasons that need no apology—the well-being of these particular teenagers is very special to me.

The weakness of my analogy is obvious because I am only a human; but I don't think it's unfitting to the Fatherhood of God. Perhaps the greatest evidence of God's paternal love is His provision of special grace through the gift of His Son, Jesus Christ, to those who wish to call Him "Father." This means that God's "indescribable gift" as Paul calls it (2 Cor. 9:15), is for those creatures who acknowledge themselves to be disobedient children, who confess their sins and turn from disobedience to honor and worship the Father.

When we do this, we find another mark of God's Fatherhood in His willingness to forgive, as the Psalmist so beautifully expresses: "He has not treated us as our sins deserve or requited us for our misdeeds. For as the heaven stands high above the earth, so His strong love stands high over all who fear Him. Far as east is from west, so far has He put our offences away from us. As a Father has compassion on his children, so has the Lord compassion on all who fear Him. For He knows how we were made, He knows full well that we are dust" (Ps. 103:10-14, NEB).

God the Father takes into account the fact of our frailty because no one knows better than God the stuff of which we are composed. He is, after all, "God the Father Almighty, Maker of heaven and earth."

"He is God," said Augustine in one of his sermons, "and He is Father: God in power, Father in goodness. How blessed we are who find that our Lord God is our Father!"

According to C. B. Armstrong, the term best expressing God is "that used by Jesus—Father: the Source of the being of persons. Faith is our approach to Him: grace is His approach to us."

The Apostles' Creed is careful, however, to avoid leaving an impression of God the Father as some doting senior citizen—a grandfather whose grandchildren exploit His senility and sentimentality. He is Almighty—*deus omnipotens* in the Latin original. When God chose to change Abram's name to Abraham, he first revealed himself as *El Shaddai,* "The Almighty God" (Gen. 17:1). This name was passed on through the generations—the God of Abraham, Isaac, and Jacob was the Lord God Almighty.

But when His people, enslaved in Egypt, most needed evidence of His power, God then chose to reveal Himself to Moses by still another name: "*I AM THAT I AM*" (Ex. 3:14). The Hebrew word we pronounce as *Yahweh* and translate *Jehovah* derives from the Hebrew verb "to be." Yahweh is a Being who by His acts in history shows Himself to be Almighty God, "the Lord strong and mighty, the Lord mighty in battle" (Ps. 24:8). Cyril of Jerusalem said, around A.D. 350, "The divine Scripture and the utterances of the truth know only One God who rules all things by His power."

Of course, one of the classic mind-bending questions is: If God is Almighty, is there anything He can't do? The Christian Church has argued over this enigma from the beginning. Augustine declared, "He is, in a word, omnipotent to perform everything He wills." But, Augustine went on to say, "I can tell the sort of things He could not do. He cannot die, He cannot sin, He cannot lie, He cannot be deceived. Such things He cannot; if He could, He would not be Almighty." The fullest and briefest summary of these restrictions on our understanding of God's omnipotence had already been given by Paul to Timothy, probably quoting an early creed: "If we are faithless, He will remain faithful, for He cannot disown Himself" (2 Tim. 2:13).

God the Creator

The final description of God in this first clause of the Apostles' Creed is "Maker of heaven and earth." God is Father, God is Almighty, God is Creator. Scholars have sometimes disputed the choice of words, "Maker" versus "Creator," but this needn't trouble us. An early creed from the Council of Chalcedon, in A.D. 451, uses the Greek word *poieten*, from which we obtain our word *poet*. The same root appears throughout the New Testament in reference to God's creative power, in Ephesians 2:10, for instance, referring to God's *workmanship* or *handiwork*. In other words, God is a poet, the Maker and Creator of:

> All things bright and beautiful,
> All creatures great and small,
> All things wise and wonderful,
> The Lord God made them all.

This is the God whom Paul introduced to the Athenians: "The God who made the world and everything in it is the Lord of heaven and earth" (Acts 17:24). He is a Being wholly self-sufficient, says Paul, "not served by human hands, as if He needed anything, because He Himself gives all men life and breath and everything else" (17:25). The 17th century hymn by John Mason expresses it this way:

> Thou wast, O Lord, and Thou wast blessed
> Before the world began;
> Of Thine eternity possessed
> Before time's hour-glass ran.
> Thou needest none Thy praise to sing,
> As if Thy joy could fade.
> Could'st Thou have needed anything,
> Thou could'st have nothing made.

Speaking about God as "Maker of heaven and earth" reminds us that He alone can lay claim to creativity. Only God created *ex nihilo*, out of nothing. Many people today take credit for being creative; major corporations designate whole blocks of employees as "the creative department"; colleges offer courses in "creative writing." These claims to creativity become usurpations of God's rightful and singular claim. For none of us who write or draw or sculpt or compose music is in any genuine sense of the word *creative*. We haven't created out of thin air the materials we work with—the paper, paint, marble, and certainly not the tones that resonate as music. What we suppose comes from within us—our ideas that we set down as poems, our vision and shape of reality, our melodies and rhythms—didn't originate with us either. Every great artist who has ever been asked the question, "Where does your inspiration come from?" has admitted that he is merely a vehicle, a recorder of something he has heard or seen within his soul. But as to where it comes from, he may not profess to know.

The Christian artist, of course, knows. He understands that God, who created the universe, endows every human being—some to greater degrees than others—wth a desire to imitate the Creator. Made in the image of God, men and women possess a God-given compulsion to keep chaos from intruding into the created world. To be made in God's image means that mankind has been empowered with *imagination.* Imagination takes existing substances or ideas and brings them together in new ways to enrich personal experience. Imagination helps man reach out into the universe or deeper inside himself in the quest for something new or a greater description of the reason for being.

Since God is Creator, He also has final authority over His creation. Someone has said, "To believe in God means that the rules will always be fair, and there will be surprises." God is dependable without being predictable. He can intervene in human affairs; He can intrude upon apparent "laws of nature" to fulfill His purpose. These surprises are what we call miracles. But whether or not God chooses to perform a miracle in our lives, the chief fact for us to remember is that He is the God of providence—*Jehovah-jireh,* "the Lord who provides" (Gen. 22:14). This universe we inhabit is neither random nor chaotic, uncaused nor accidental. For the Christian, to say "I believe in God the Father Almighty, Maker of heaven and earth" means trusting in the God who provides for His creation and especially for His children.

3

*". . . And in Jesus Christ His
only Son our Lord . . ."*

By all standards, the name chosen for a child ought
to suggest something of his parents' hope and expectation. Some parents purchase a handbook of
name meanings, as a guide to selecting an offspring's name.

Neither Mary nor Joseph, of course, had any
choice in the matter. They were both told (see
Luke 1:31) what the infant's name was to be. And
to that name—Jesus or "Saviour"—a shocking new
meaning was attributed.

"You are to give Him the name Jesus, because He
will save His people from their sins." So the angel
informed Joseph (Matt. 1:21) of the impending
birth and naming of the Baby.

By the unusual circumstances of this birth,
Joseph and Mary must have realized that the Child
would be different from others. Many families in
Israel may have hoped that a deliverer from Roman
oppression might spring from them. But to be the
Saviour from *sins*? Here was a Saviour indeed! No
wonder we read that "Mary treasured up all these
things and pondered them in her mind" (Luke

2:19). She would have been adding blasphemy to scandal to do otherwise.

The great series of clauses found in the center of the Apostles' Creed rightly focuses on the central doctrine of the Christian Church—the redemption of the human race provided by God the Father through His Son and confirmed by the presence of the Holy Spirit. Once more, in affirming what the Creed declares, I am committing myself to belief *in* the Person known for 2,000 years as Jesus of Nazareth; the Person anticipated for centuries earlier as "God's Anointed One." I'm not merely asserting the fact of His historical existence, important as that is. I'm ascribing to Him qualities of uniqueness and authority granted to no one else.

Jesus' Name

Jesus is an anglicized variation on the Hebrew name *Yeshua* or *Joshua*. It means "saviour." As a name for ordinary Jewish men, it wasn't an especially sacred name. Presumably it was chosen in most instances in honor of Moses' successor who led the Israelites into Canaan. (For other instances of the name, see Ezra 2:2; 3:2; Hag. 1:2ff; Zech. 3:1ff; Acts 13:6; and Col. 4:11.)

He was Jesus of Nazareth to His contemporaries, "the son, so it was thought, of Joseph" (Luke 3:23); see also Luke 4:22; John 1:45; and John 6:42). It wasn't until the momentous occasion at Caesarea Philippi (Matt. 16:13-20; Mark 8:27-33; Luke 9:18-22), when Simon Peter identified Jesus of Nazareth as the long-awaited Messiah, that He became known as "Jesus the Christ."

Messiah means "God's Anointed" in the particular sense of a chosen representative or messenger.

Remember how the prophet Samuel designated first Saul, then David, to be king? (See 1 Sam. 10:1ff and 16:1-13.) But the prophets of Israel spoke longingly of a greater king than King David, anticipated as the Messenger who would bring to completion the revelation of God's truth. *Christ,* from the Greek word *Christos,* carries with it the same meaning. When Peter said, "You are the Christ," he was summing up in a word the hopes and prayers of men throughout history.

The Messiah as God's Messenger brings with Him the message of deliverance, the Good News of freedom. But because that Good News is personified in the very Messenger who brings it, He is the Word Himself—the liberating Word come to set us free. He is Jesus Christ,

the Name that charms our fears,

that bids our sorrows cease

because by the very power of God in Jesus Christ,

He breaks the power of reigning sin,

He sets the prisoner free.

But it's essential for us to realize that to avail ourselves of this Good News—this Gospel of freedom—we must first join Peter in recognizing who Jesus is. As Jesus of Nazareth, He was merely an itinerant teacher to whom remarkable gifts have been attributed. This is the spirit in which His fellow townsmen viewed Him (see Luke 4:14ff), in which King Herod found his curiosity piqued (see Luke 23:8). To leave Jesus classified as anything less than "the Messiah, the Son of the living God" is to make Gamaliel's comparison with Theudas or Judas the Galilean (see Acts 5:34-39). He must be known as Jesus Christ, in order to be Jesus the Lord.

This is the truth at the very heart of Simon Peter's sermon at the Feast of Pentecost. He began by introducing the crowd to Jesus of Nazareth, "a man accredited by God to you by miracles, wonders and signs" (Acts 2:22). He reminded them of the Crucifixion, just fifty days previous, and then announced the fact of the Resurrection. He called upon David's prophecy in Psalm 16:8 as evidence that the true Anointed of God should not be subject to death. Then Peter linked together the two strands of his argument: the patriarch's prophecy and the fact that Jesus of Nazareth had been dead and was now alive again! It cannot be other than what Peter declared: "Therefore, let all Israel be assured of this: God has made this Jesus whom you crucified both Lord and Christ" (Acts 2:36).

So went the preaching throughout the early days of the new Church. Every time Peter had a chance to speak, his message was essentially the same: Jesus of Nazareth is the Messiah, the Christ, of which fact the Resurrection stands as incontrovertible proof. In consequence, Peter was able to assert the uniqueness of Jesus of Nazareth: He is God's only choice through whom to reveal Himself to human beings. He is the only means of access to God the Father, the only source of salvation from this present corruption (see Acts 2:37ff). On a later occasion, the Apostle spoke even more directly: "Salvation is found in no one else; for there is no other name under heaven given to men by which we must be saved" (Acts 4:12).

The point Peter made—and the Apostles' Creed reinforces—is that, if Jesus of Nazareth is indeed risen from the dead, then He must be the Christ, the Messiah, God's Anointed Messenger. As such,

He holds exclusively the power from God the Father to grant deliverance and redemption to the human race.

Jesus the Son of God

This exclusive claim to be God's Messenger is further supported by the next phrase of the Apostles' Creed, ". . . His only Son." Scholars studying how the Creed expanded from a few simple expressions to its present form report that the "only Son" phrase is a relatively late addition. No doubt the phrase was added specifically to combat heresies springing up in the early centuries. Among these false teachings was the heresy that Jesus was merely one of many sons of God.

Of course, the New Testament offers ample evidence that Jesus taught and the apostles believed that He was *the* Son of God. The notable example from Matthew's account occurred when Jesus invited Peter to walk on the water, as He Himself was doing (see Matt. 14:25-33). When they returned to the boat, "those who were in the boat worshiped Him, saying, 'Truly You are the Son of God'" (Matt. 14:33). Other references cite the recognition by demon-possessed persons, as in Mark 3:11 or Luke 4:41, "You are the Son of God!" After hearing the Good News from the Apostle Philip, the Ethiopian treasurer confessed his faith in unequivocal words: "I believe that Jesus Christ is the Son of God" (Acts 8:37, KJV). And the newly converted Saul of Tarsus had only one sermon in his first few days as a believer: "At once he began to preach in the synagogues that Jesus is the Son of God" (Acts 9:20).

This evidence continues throughout the New

Testament to show that the Early Church held, from the beginning, that Jesus of Nazareth was the Son of God incarnate. Whatever skepticism may have clouded their perception at the Crucifixion, the apostles found it dispelled by the Resurrection, as we most assuredly know from the witness of Thomas (see John 20:24-29). The apostolic writers are unabashed about the claim they made. As Paul stated, the man Jesus "was declared with power to be the Son of God by His resurrection from the dead: Jesus Christ our Lord" (Rom. 1:4).

The Uniqueness of Jesus

But it's in the later writings of the Apostle John that we find an emphasis on the *only*-ness of the Son. In particular, John seems to have been opposing the heresy known as gnosticism. The gnostics taught—among other false teachings—that since matter is evil, the Son of God could not have appeared in physical form. Therefore, either Jesus was not the Son of God, or else Jesus was spirit and not flesh.

In the prologue to his Gospel, John declares that "the Word became flesh and lived for a while among us. We have seen His glory, the glory of the one and only Son, who came from the Father" (John 1:14). Here he asserts both the physical nature and the uniqueness of the Son. A few sentences later, he writes, "No one has ever seen God; but God the only Son, who is at the Father's side, He has made Him known" (John 1:18).

Perhaps the most beloved verse in the New Testament is John 3:16, where again the singularity of the Son stands out: "For God so loved the world that He gave His one and only Son, that whoever believes in Him shall not perish but have everlasting life."

God's unselfishness is sometimes overlooked by our exultant joy at the wealth of His gift. The fact is, to give us eternal life, God first had to give up His only Son. As a result of so great an act of selfless giving, humanity is faced by a special obligation not to disdain it. Believing in God's gift of life means believing in—acknowledging with all due honor—"the name of God's one and only Son" (John 3:18).

Finally, in his first epistle, the aged Apostle John reiterates his theme. "This is how God showed His love among us: He sent His one and only Son into the world that we might live through Him" (1 John 4:9).

Who, then, is Jesus? He is the Saviour, sent by God to save men and women from their sins. He is Christ, the Messiah, God's Word-in-flesh to the human race. He shares this glory with no one else because He is "God's one and only Son." This is why we read, from the great hymn of praise, quoted by Paul in Philippians, that "at the name of Jesus every knee should bow, in heaven and on earth and under the earth, and every tongue confess that Jesus Christ is Lord, to the glory of God the Father" (Phil. 2:10-11).

The Lordship of Jesus

"I believe . . . in Jesus Christ His only Son *our Lord.*" Saviour, Messiah, and Son, to be sure. But Jesus of Nazareth is also Lord of the universe. He is the Word who, before all Creation, spoke the will of the Father and illumined the cosmos with the light of the Spirit. He called the world into being.

By His authority the universe holds together, for as the author of the letter to the Hebrews tells us, "the Son is . . . sustaining all things by His powerful word" (Heb. 1:3).

The Lordship of Jesus Christ is the theme of Paul's letter to the Colossians. Paul quotes what many New Testament scholars believe to be another hymn from the Early Church. "He is the image of the invisible God, the Firstborn over all creation. For by Him all things were created: things in heaven and on earth, visible and invisible, whether thrones or powers or rulers or authorities; all things were created by Him and for Him. He is before all things, and in Him all things hold together" (Col. 1:15-17).

Many marvelous truths shine in this passage. For instance, the contrast between *image* and *invisible*: the one, an exact physical representation; the other, the unseeable. In Jesus Christ, we have all that may be known of God, because as Paul also says, "For God was pleased to have all His fullness dwell in Him" (Col. 1:19). Thus Jesus Christ makes known to us in His Person the God who otherwise veils Himself in glory.

Another truth: Jesus Christ, as the Firstborn, is thereby privileged with the absolute rights to inherit all His Father's estate. As "God's one and only Son," this is His right. But if the word *Firstborn* is to have its logical meaning, later sons must also be born. So there will be, as Paul teaches in Romans 8 and Galatians 4. But while both the Father and the Son are willing to share the inheritance with us, there is never to be any doubt as to the primacy of the Firstborn.

The Son through whom the Father chooses to reveal Himself is the sovereign Lord of Creation, with authority over every echelon and hierarchy. This truth was but dimly perceived by the Twelve Apostles until after the Resurrection—although it had been understood by a centurion at Capernaum (see Luke 7:1-10). Having heard that Jesus of Nazareth had mastery over the elements of nature, over disease and even death, it wasn't hard for the Roman officer to put faith in the Master to heal an outsider. The centurion realized that faith begins with a recognition of the sovereignty of God. So, reasoning by analogy (A is to B as C is to D), he told Jesus that just as an officer can issue orders and expect them to be obeyed, so Jesus could exercise His authority, merely by speaking the word. Yet only God can speak to the wind and waves, to atoms and particles, to bacteria and chromosomes. It is this supremely divine power and authority that the Roman officer identified with none other than Jesus of Nazareth Himself!

Furthermore, Jesus Christ is Lord over all—all spheres and dimensions of the cosmos, including the many galaxies and stellar systems still beyond our comprehension. He is Lord over every asteroid and comet. Wherever life may exist, in whatever form or on whatever scale, the eternal Word who became flesh in our history and on our planet as Jesus of Nazareth is Lord over that life as well. The novels of C. S. Lewis—*Out of the Silent Planet, Perelandra,* and *That Hideous Strength*—may be helpful in enlarging our imagination to comprehend the limitless Lordship of Jesus Christ.

He is also Lord over every element in this realm as well. He is Lord over climate and catastrophe, Lord over politics and diplomacy, Lord over war and peace, Lord over economics and social development, Lord over education, Lord over the arts, Lord over science, Lord over recreation and sport, Lord over health and the span of every individual life.

Jesus Christ is also the sustaining Lord of the universe, holding all things together in Himself. Sometimes we allow a crude caricature of this truth to invade our minds, seeing the sustaining power of the Lord Jesus Christ like some kind of sanctified Elmer's Glue-All. Instead, He is the very center of the cosmos He created. He is its focal point, its fulcrum, its integrating principle.

But the Lordship of Jesus Christ isn't an advanced doctrine we can afford to leave for the more intellectual among us. Nowhere does the Scripture teach or allow by neglect the insidious notion that we can honor Jesus as Saviour, Jesus as Messiah or Christ, but not Jesus as Lord. Nowhere are we permitted to assume one relationship while ignoring the other. The very punctuation of the Apostles' Creed should help us to see this fact. It doesn't say, interrupted by commas, *And in Jesus, Christ, His only Son, our Lord.* It says, without any subordination or division, *And in Jesus Christ His only Son our Lord.*

The preaching of the apostles after the Resurrection gives Jesus Christ His full due. The favorite creedal statement in the New Testament ascribes to Him full honor: He is the Lord Jesus Christ! So too, we must believe Him to be.

Historical Aspects
Some early Latin creeds reversed the present word order to say, "And in Christ Jesus His only Son our

Lord." Historian J. N. D. Kelly has suggested that this Latin version shows how much Western Christianity still relied upon Jewish influences. In the second and third centuries, it was essential to make the connection between the Jews' expectation of a Messiah and that fulfillment in the Person of Jesus of Nazareth.

The word for *Christ* itself needed no explanation. That had been amply provided by Justin Martyr in the year A.D. 161 when before the Roman Senate he identified the *Christos* with the *logos*—the Messenger with the Message!

This is still important today, even though the Gospel reaches beyond the hope of Israel, encompassing all humanity throughout all of history. We give primacy, therefore, to the name of Jesus, to His identity as a man in history. As Oscar Cullman has written concerning the Gospel of John, "If one speaks of Jesus, one speaks of history. The theological assertion contained in the word *Christ* is connected, then, with Jesus, with history. Faith in the Jesus of history as the *Christ* is what the evangelist seeks to impart to his readers."

4

" . . . Who was conceived by the Holy Ghost, born of the Virgin Mary: Suffered under Pontius Pilate, was crucified, dead, and buried: He descended into hell . . ."

It seems so simple; yet far too many Christians have allowed a sort of Christmas-card sentimentality to govern their thinking. Grotesque as it seems, their pre-historic "Jesus" does some kind of miniaturization to compress Himself into the body of an infant. The theological fact must be more precisely stated. The eternal Word, co-eternal with the Father and the Spirit, emptied Himself of His divine glory, divested Himself of His properties as spirit, and became flesh in the fetus of a male child supernaturally conceived in Mary's womb.

This supernatural conception is no more or less miraculous than the birth of the universe, for it was the same creative power of the Holy Spirit that first responded to the will of the Father and the word of the Son: *"Fiat Lux!* Let there be light!" No one who believes that God could create the universe should stumble at the doctrine of the Incarnation.

In this chapter we deal with the clauses of the Apostles' Creed which present the great truth of the Incarnation—the taking on of human form in flesh and blood by that preexistent member of the

Triune Godhead whose eternal name is the Word—
and the living out of that life in our space and time.

Before the Incarnation

At the very outset, we need to be clear on several
matters relating to divine preexistence and the Incarnation. Various passages of Scripture teach us
to believe in the eternal interrelationship of the
Godhead before time, before Creation. (See Prov.
8:22-31, for instance.) This relationship is to be
understood as the Trinity's dwelling in perfect
unity as spirit. The Trinity always acts in consort.
The Genesis accounts of Creation and of the Tower
of Babel both use the plural pronoun *Us* to express
a divine decision: "Let Us make man" and "Come,
let Us go down, and there confound their language"
(Gen. 1:26 and 11:7). In the first instance, the
Father wills; the Son speaks; the Spirit illumines.
In the second case, the Father wills; the Son with-
draws the Word; the Spirit darkens the minds of
men.

But there was no Jesus of Nazareth present in
heaven on Creation Day or at the Plain of Shinar.
Indeed, no one known as Jesus of Nazareth existed
till, once again, the Father willed and the quicken-
ing Spirit acted, this time within the womb of a
young woman named Mary. When the Word once
more spoke, it was as a Man.

Reasonable Questions

Still, there are two reasonable questions many
people ask: *How?* and *Why?* The first is Mary's
own question. The authenticity of her angelic visita-
tion and its startling message is proved by this fact
above all others: When she was told that she would

conceive and bear a son, she had common sense enough to ask how she, a virgin, could give birth to anyone. She also realized that no child born of her eventual lawful union with Joseph could merit the name of Israel's long-expected Messiah, the Son of God.

The answer given to Mary, however, was direct and uncomplicated: "The Holy Spirit will come upon you, and the power of the Most High will overshadow you. So the holy one to be born will be called the Son of God" (Luke 1:35). The same explanation given to Joseph (see Matt. 1:18-25) confirms that the Holy Spirit is responsible for implanting the life-seed which is to give birth to the Word-made-flesh.

The second question is *Why?* Why did God choose such a bizarre method of revealing Himself to the human race? Why did He allow the humiliation of human birth to trammel Him with physical needs and appetites, weariness and pain, swiftly passing time, the faithlessness of family and friends, and finally the wretchedness of betrayal and an unjust execution?

A story is told about a husband who had taken his wife to a Christmas Eve service at the church she attended. He'd refused to stay himself, however, because he rejected the idea of God becoming Man. "I can't respect a God who would want to give up being God to become like me," he told his wife.

As he returned home, a heavy snow was falling, and on his front lawn a flock of winter birds huddled against the storm. Their wings were so burdened down with snow, they could scarcely fly. A wave of compassion for the helpless birds swept through the man, and he went into his house to bring the birds some bread. But as he approached them, they scattered in fright, hopping and flitting away.

"If they don't eat, they'll die," the man said to himself. "I've got to get food to them somehow." Then addressing the birds he said, "Don't be afraid. I want to help you. I want to save you. If only I could communicate with you. If only, for a moment, I could explain to you—but to do that, I'd have to become one of you . . ."

And then he realized the meaning of the Incarnation!

Why did God take on human form? We can't begin to answer fully so large a question. It's the subject of some of the Bible's most demanding texts. In one such passage, Hebrews 1—2, the writer explains the nature of the Son of God's eternal glory in His pre-Incarnational state, and some of the reasons for abandoning that glory. Briefly, the Incarnation represents God's means of demonstrating once and for all His desire to be our Father. Then all members of the same family who share the same experience of human life, its terror of death, can also share the glorious triumph over death that only God could provide.

To achieve all this, the writer tells us, it was necessary that God Himself take part in what it means to be human, in order to ratify for Himself that which He had once created and called good. So, we read, "in bringing many sons to glory, it was fitting that God, for whom and through whom everything exists, should make the Pioneer of their salvation perfect through suffering" (Heb. 2:10). Don't be bothered by that word "perfect." It doesn't mean that the Word-made-flesh in the Person of Jesus was sinful and *imp*erfect. The Greek word here translated "perfect" means more nearly "brought to a condition of fullness, whereby no further development or experience is necessary." In other words, until God-in-Christ died, Christ hadn't experienced every aspect of what it was to be human!

But now, says the writer of Hebrews, that's all been changed. "Since the children have flesh and blood, He too shared in their humanity so that by His death He might destroy him who holds the power of death—that is, the devil—and free those who all their lives were held in slavery by their fear of death" (Heb. 2:14-15).

Thus the Apostles' Creed affirms that the Lord Jesus Christ, who is none other than the only begotten Son of God, is also fully human. He is no bionic man, no preternatural freak.

The Miraculous Conception

The fact that Jesus' conception bypassed the normal male procreative function means only this: God ordained that the Word-made-flesh should be free from the congenital state of sinfulness all other men and women inherit as descendants of Adam. "God the Father Almighty, Maker of heaven and earth" certainly had it in His power to enact what C. S. Lewis calls "the grand miracle," God becoming man.

Of course, the miraculous conception of the Word in the womb of a virgin always elicits scoffing. As Lewis also says in his well-known book *Miracles,*

The idea that the progress of science has somehow altered this question is closely bound up with the idea that people "in olden times" believed in [miracles] "because they didn't know the laws of Nature." Thus you will hear people say, "The early Christians believed that Christ was the son of a virgin, but we know that this is a scientific impossibility." Such people seem to have an idea that belief in miracles arose at a period when men were so ignorant of the course of nature that they did not perceive a miracle to be contrary to it. A moment's thought shows this to be nonsense: and the story of the Virgin Birth is a particularly striking example. When St. Joseph discovered that his fiancée was going to have a baby, he not unnaturally decided to repudiate her. Why? Because he knew just as well as any modern gynecologist that in the ordinary course of nature women do not have babies unless they have lain with men. No doubt the modern gynecologist knows several things about birth and begetting which St. Joseph did not know. But those things do not concern the main point—that a virgin birth is contrary to the course of nature. And St. Joseph obviously knew *that*. In any sense in which it is true to say now, "The thing is scientifically impossible," he would have said the same: the thing always was, and was always known to be, impossible *unless* the regular processes of nature were, in this particular case, being overruled or supplemented by something from beyond nature. When St. Joseph finally accepted the view that his fiancée's pregnancy was due not to unchastity but to a miracle, he accepted the miracle as something contrary to the known order of nature.[1]

Jesus' Birth

As to the birth itself, we have no record in Scripture causing us to assume that it was in any way other than normal. Certainly the location was inconvenient and the witnesses somewhat extraordinary; but Mary's full term ended in labor and delivery of the most natural kind. And while the life and ministry of the man known as Jesus of Nazareth included, in Peter's words, "miracles, wonders and signs, which God did among you through Him" (Acts 2:22), that life was otherwise entirely human in its need for food, shelter, rest, companionship, affection, and love. To believe anything less is to make Jesus into some kind of mythic hero, a demigod like Hercules, instead of "the Man Christ Jesus" (1 Tim. 2:5).

In his teaching to the Galatians, Paul shows this to be true. "God sent His Son," he writes, "born of a woman, born under the law" (Gal. 4:4). The Son of God permitted Himself to become subject to all the governing forces of this world; to be born in helpless dependence upon a mother's love and care. Hence, He was subject to laws of natural experience—such as the fact that fire burns, water quenches thirst, or disappointment causes anguish.

Jesus' Death

Interestingly, the Apostles' Creed has nothing to say about this phase of Jesus' life. There is no ap-

---

[1] C. S. Lewis, *Miracles: A Preliminary Study* (New York: Macmillan Publishing Company, 1963), pp. 47-48.

parent concern about validating the miracles or summarizing His teaching. Instead, the Creed moves directly to His suffering and death. However, a most important point is made. "Suffered *under Pontius Pilate*" is more than an accusatory reminder of that politician's moral weakness. It serves as a means of historical verification.

Ancient dating depended largely upon reckoning from the year of a ruler's coronation to his death. For example, Luke dates the beginning of John the Baptist's ministry this way: "In the fifteenth year of the reign of Tiberius Caesar when Pontius Pilate was governor of Judea, when Herod was tetrarch of Galilee, . . . during the high priesthood of Annas and Caiaphas, the word of God came to John son of Zechariah in the desert" (Luke 3:1-2). To anyone interested, we can now discover that Tiberius Julius Caesar, adopted son of the emperor Augustus, succeeded as emperor of Rome in September, in the year A.D. 14. "In the fifteenth year," therefore, dates John's beginning at A.D. 29.

The first Christians carefully dated their history. Ignatius, Bishop of Antioch, writing to Smyrna around A.D. 100, speaks of Jesus Christ as "truly nailed for us in the flesh in the times of Pontius Pilate and Herod the Tetrarch." Perhaps 50 years later, Justin Martyr wrote a treatise called *The First Apology,* addressed to the Emperor Antonius Pius and his adopted sons, Marcus Aurelius and Lucius Verus. In this document, Justin Martyr also notes that Jesus had been crucified "under Pontius Pilate, who was governor in Judea in the days of Tiberius Caesar."

The commentator Rufinus, in A.D. 404, wrote, "Those who handed down the Creed showed great wisdom in underlining the actual date at which these things happened, so that there might be no chance of any uncertainty or vagueness upsetting the stability of the tradition."

The four Gospel writers treat rather matter-of-factly their accounts of the Crucifixion, perhaps because death on a cross was a form of punishment well-known by all their contemporaries. To citizens and subjects of the Roman Empire, death by crucifixion was a common spectacle. It was nothing new. Five hundred years before Jesus' death, the Persian Darius had crucified 3,000 enemies at one time. The Carthaginians taught the Romans to use crucifixion for purposes of intimidation. They lined roads with crosses in much the same way old English cross-roads still display the gibbets of two centuries ago.

But while a crucifixion may have been routine for those who viewed it, the victim knew its special horror. *The Day Christ Died* by Jim Bishop offers a detailed description of the execution in all its brutality. We use the word *excruciating*, meaning "derived from the experience of the cross," to describe agonizing pain. Yet while none of its suffering can be exaggerated, the fact remains that the cross' greatest cause of anguish may not have been the nails impaling the hands and feet. The greater cause may have been its shame.

To die on a cross was to be exposed for hours, in rare instances for days, to the taunting scorn of mobs. While the victim struggled to breathe, shifting his weight from dangling by his hands to pressing upon his feet—while his pectoral muscles collapsed, suffocating him—there was not even the dignity of privacy. Stripped naked (and we must hereafter ignore the delicate sensibilities of painters showing Jesus draped with a loincloth), the condemned could only wait out their agony. Some chose silence. Others cursed their fate and those who mocked them.

This is the death of which the Creed speaks, the death to which the Son of God was subjected. It's a death so ignominious, Paul refers to it as something too outrageous, too shameful to consider. It is nothing short of scandalous, that "being found in appearance as a man, He humbled Himself and became obedient to death—even death on a cross!" (Phil. 2:8). The mechanics of expression in this statement indicate amazement that the humiliation of God should lower Him to such a degree.

We need to rid ourselves of sentimental notions when we speak of the Cross. Too often we have glamorized it, turning the Cross into a pretty ornament. We have sung songs idolatrous and even blasphemous in their theological sloppiness. We ought not to "cherish the old rugged Cross." It isn't our "Statue of Liberty," as one modern song claims. The Cross is the intersecting point where God met mankind, accepted the worst abuse man could offer, and stretching out His arms in love, offered forgiveness. But the Cross remains a symbol of consummate passions intertwined—love mixed with hatred, with love prevailing.

The Cross is also the place where the Word-made-flesh redeemed mankind from sin. The word in Greek for "redeem" suggests going to the marketplace and paying a price, as if for a slave. The slave can't free himself; someone else must accomplish this on his behalf. Redemption is paid for us by the one who thereafter, in love, claims us for His own.

The Apostles' Creed declares Jesus to have been "crucified, dead, and buried" because an early and persistent heresy called Docetism taught that Jesus had never really died. Several ingenious explanations attempted to do away with the witness of Nicodemus, Joseph of Arimathea, and others present at the removal of Jesus' body from the cross and its subsequent entombment (see John 19:28-42). One theory was that Jesus merely seemed to be dead, having entered into a state of suspended animation. Another theory, much more melodramatic, offered a last minute substitute: Judas Iscariot repented just in time to take Jesus' place, or else Simon of Cyrene, conscripted to carry the cross, was then compelled to die upon it.

Quite apart from opposing these errors, the Creed's declarations of Jesus' death and burial also prepare for and give meaning to the grand climax of the Resurrection. Without real death and burial, there can be no reasonable explanation for the Resurrection claims.

Jesus' Descent into Hell

The final clause in this sequence, "He descended into hell," is the most controversial in the Apostles' Creed. Indeed, some denominations consider it optional or refuse to include it at all. The problem with this phrase begins with what it connotes. To some, the descent into hell represents the physical agony of death upon the Cross. It was hellish in its pain. To others, the word *hell* means *Hades* or *Sheol*, the collective abode of the dead, divided into Paradise or Abraham's Bosom—the state of God-fearing souls—and *Gehenna*, the state of ungodly souls. Thus the descent into hell may suggest that the Son of God carried the sins of the world to hell; or the Son of God carried the Good News of deliverance to the godly dead such as Lazarus the beggar and the repentant thief. A third-century Syrian creed speaks of Jesus, "who was crucified under Pontius Pilate and departed in peace, in order to preach to Abraham, Isaac, and Jacob and all the saints concerning the ending of the world and the resurrection of the dead."

Still others believe that the descent into hell accounts for the problem of God's justice by providing an opportunity for all mankind—in eternity as well as in time—to hear the message of redemption from the Word Himself. But whatever interpretation one accepts, the scriptural passages upon which this teaching is based must be studied closely. Some of the standard texts are Job 38:17, Psalm 68:18-22, Matthew 12:38-41, Acts 2:22-32, Romans 10:7, Ephesians 4:7-10, 1 Peter 3:18-20, and 1 Peter 4:6.

5

*". . . The third day He rose again
from the Dead . . ."*

The resurrection of Jesus Christ is the keystone of
Christianity. Remove from history the fact of His
literal, physical, bodily coming-to-life-again, explain it away, account for it as wish-fulfillment or
the power of suggestion—and the whole story of
God coming to earth as Man, the Word-made-flesh,
becomes nonsense. Unless the God who made the
world has power over death, He certainly is not
the Almighty. In such a case, the Man Jesus was an
imposter, and no more Lord than you or I.

So when Christians affirm their belief in the Resurrection, we advance the Creed to its most radical
and fundamental point. Here we take our stand on
an issue which is rooted in the very truth of God.
Until this clause, the Creed—by some stretching of
language—might be subject to occasional variant
interpretations: the metaphor of God as Father,
the martyrdom of Jesus as an example of brotherly
love. But when it comes to resurrection from bloody
physical death, there is no room for figures of
speech. As the poet John Updike says, in "Seven
Stanzas at Easter,"

Let us not mock God with metaphor,
analogy, sidestepping, transcendence;
making of the event a parable, a sign painted
    in the faded credulity of ages:
let us walk through the door.[1]

The Power of the Resurrection

When we accept the poet's invitation and "walk through the door," what do we find? We find that if God is Maker of heaven and earth, if the Word called the world into being out of nothing, and if the Spirit brought divine energy into the works of Creation, then *nothing* is impossible for such a God. He has power to recall to life the Son whom He so willingly gave to save us from our sins.

This is a magnificent phrase in the Apostle Paul's letter to the Philippians: "I want to know Christ and the power of His resurrection" (3:10). That power shows itself in most remarkable ways. First, it identifies Jesus of Nazareth as the unique Man in history. Many persons, widely known in their lifetimes, have appeared to influence the world—Hammurabi, Alexander the Great, Julius Caesar. But to each of them, and to all men, has come the fact of death. Thereafter, these great heroes live on in memory and nothing more. Even their monuments, so carefully constructed to preserve the glory of their achievements, crumble and decay. The poem "Ozymandias" by Percy Shelley speaks for all of them:

    I met a traveler from an antique land
    Who said: Two vast and trunkless legs of stone

---

[1] From John Updike, *Telephone Poles and Other Poems* (New York: Alfred A. Knopf, Inc., 1963). Used by permission.

Stand in the desert. Near them, on the sand,
Half sunk, a shattered visage lies, whose frown,
And wrinkled lip, and sneer of cold command,
Tell that its sculptor well those passions read
Which yet survive, stamped on these lifeless
    things,
The hand that mocked them, and the heart
    that fed;
And on the pedestal these words appear:
"My name is Ozymandias, king of kings:
Look on my works, ye mighty, and despair!"
Nothing beside remains. Round the decay
Of that colossal wreck, boundless and bare,
The lone and level sands stretch far away.

Collectively, all the famous men and women of history have failed to alter human experience as much as did Jesus of Nazareth. He wrote no books, He enacted no laws, He led no armies; but His conquest over death sets Him apart and calls forth expressions of allegiance from every tribe, people, tongue, and nation.

Because of the power of the Resurrection, history must be reckoned by taking into account the Person of Jesus. We record events in reference to Him: they happened either B.C., before Christ, or A.D., *anno domini*, "in the year of the Lord." Other calendars exist, to be sure. In the State of Israel, dates before Christ are spoken of as having occurred "B.C.E.," meaning "before the Common Era." What makes our era *common* is the universal recognition that history is measured in relationship to the life of Jesus of Nazareth.

By the power of His resurrection, Jesus Christ is Lord over human history, determining that its events should be subordinate to Him. That same power also governs our lives at a level of experience so frequent and so customary, we may well have ceased to recognize it.

The First Day of the Week

In pagan North America, one Sunday is pretty much like any other, depending on what professional sport happens to be in season. It's mostly a day to recuperate from the working-week's losses, to store up sufficient energy to face the new week's chores. Without really knowing or caring where the idea of Sunday's rest came from, the unchurched family settles in to a routine of morning lethargy, brunch, an afternoon and evening of television or recreation. Recently, in many parts of the United States and Canada, even the relaxation emphasis of a secular Sunday is being swallowed up in greed as department stores and shopping malls open seven days for business.

A Christian family has opportunities to experience a far different quality in the same day. *Sunday:* Not the last day of the weekend, as most secular-minded people would say, but the first day of the week. By our calendar, Sunday is the day on which the resurrection of Jesus of Nazareth occurred. It is the day on which His fearful and despondent followers first saw Him alive again; the day on which He showed Himself to Thomas and to the two companions walking to Emmaus. Sunday is the day set aside by early Christians for worship, fellowship, and collection of offerings (see Acts 20:7, 1 Cor. 16:2).

From these personal encounters between the risen Lord and one or two of His disciples, then with the whole number "on the first day of the week," stemmed the tradition which the Apostle John calls "the Lord's Day" (Rev. 1:10). We know, from reading the early chapters of the Book of the Acts of the Apostles, that daily meetings occurred while the Church was still localized in Jerusalem. But with persecution and dispersion, the custom of weekly meetings for worship grew. Gradually, the first day, known throughout the Roman World as "the Day of the Sun," became *dies dominica* in Latin—"the day of the Lord." In every other Western European language, the day's name in common use is derived from the same meaning: *domingo* in Spanish, *dimanche* in French.

The Lord's Day thus became the weekly celebration of the Resurrection. Even the Russian word for the first day makes this plain. *Voskresenye* comes from the word for "resurrection." The day was a festival marked by joy in the sharing of the essential Christian truth that the Lord is risen indeed. By continuing each Sunday the supper of bread and wine instituted by Jesus, and by calling it "the Lord's Supper" (1 Cor. 11:20), the Church added further sanctity to the day of its common observance.

In Justin Martyr's time, midway through the second century, a pattern for honoring the Lord's Day had been established. Justin Martyr wrote, "On the day called the Day of the Sun, all our people living in town or country meet together in one place. The memoirs of the Apostles are read, or the writings of the prophets." Then, according to Justin Martyr, a sermon followed by prayer and the singing of hymns. Last came the Lord's supper, by this time called the *Eucharist,* meaning "the favor or grace of God."

For 300 years, Christians celebrated the Resurrection on the Lord's Day without any special dispensation excusing them from work. The Day of the Sun was a business day in Rome; therefore, Christian worship occurred early in the morning, before sunrise, or late at night. But in A.D. 321, Emperor Constantine introduced the first legislation declaring Sunday a day of rest from labor for most workers, except farmers, and a day of worship for Christians. Later laws restricting activities on the Lord's Day were enforced upon all persons, believers or not. Thus some of the traditions of rest and quiet, which were known in North America until a generation or so ago, came into practice.

Of course, today much of that tradition has vanished in the pell-mell rush toward pleasure and in religious indifference toward strict Sunday observance. Even among many professing Christians there seems to be an absence of the elementary awareness of the Lord's Day as an ongoing witness to the world.

By setting aside the first day of the week and by keeping it, not for play but for renewed personal commitment to Jesus Christ as Lord, the Christian is declaring something positive. Week by week, by actions as well as by words, every Christian who observes the Lord's Day reiterates the Creed, "I believe . . . He rose again from the dead."

The Celebration of Easter

Remarkably, the story of the Resurrection penetrates into that stronghold of secularism we recognize as North American materialism. For on an appointed day, a Sunday in late March or April, in homes all over this continent, reminders of the new life available through the resurrection power of Jesus Christ will intrude upon disbelieving and uninterested minds. Emphasis is placed upon life being resurrected after the deadness of winter. And even television programs portray the life of Jesus Christ—climaxing at the empty tomb.

Because this annual celebration occurs, at least in our northern latitudes, at the beginning of spring, we can say with the Hebrew poet, "For lo, the winter is past, . . . the flowers appear on the earth; the time for the singing of birds is come" (Song, 2:11-12). We feel a freedom from winter's chill; we sense a rebirth of life in nature, perhaps even in ourselves. From all known history, mankind has celebrated the reawakening of the earth to signify his own highest aspiration—the chance to start all over again. Early Britons honored a goddess known to them as Eostre; from them we have adopted the word *Easter* and some of their festivities to rejoice in nature's new life.

But others that same day will greet the sunrise for a different reason. Not to celebrate the vernal equinox; not to follow Peter Cottontail hopping down the bunny trail; not to congratulate each other's taste in high fashion. For Christians, the day known to the world as Easter commemorates the fact of the empty tomb, the resurrection of Jesus Christ.

But unlike the frivolities of egg rolling and the Easter parade on Fifth Avenue, the Christian observance runs a risk. For if Christians take seriously the purpose and meaning of our holy day, the occasion can turn into an outrage, a scandal to the secular-minded world around us. Not because the world despises Jesus of Nazareth; quite to the contrary. A few months earlier, our shopping centers, our media and mail, were full of reminders of the Babe in Bethlehem. Only two days before, much of the business world respected Christ's memory enough to permit employees time off work for Good Friday meditation. The cross of Christ has become, quite unlike its original symbolic meaning, a beautiful emblem to be worn without shame, or a sign to dominate the skyline of our bankrupt and crime-ridden cities.

Of course, to speak of Jesus' birth may be cuddly and cute; to honor His death may be morally ennobling. But to mention the Resurrection is quite another matter. The idea of a corpse no longer dead offends human reason and wrenches us away from sentimental representations. Instead, the Resurrection confronts us with claims about the awesome and awful power of God.

The Biblical Record

In all the accounts of the Resurrection in the four Gospels, the first to discover that Jesus was risen were women. Several interesting points come to mind as we contemplate what this means. First, the four narratives agree that a huge boulder had been set up against the entrance to the sepulchre, a rock too massive for a few women to dislodge. Therefore the fact that the tomb was opened at all can't be countered by claiming that Mary Magdalene and her friends moved the stone.

Furthermore, while Jesus' own disciples may have doubted Him, His enemies remembered His prophecy that He would rise from the dead (see Matt. 27:62-66). So they informed Pilate of the consequences, should some scheme succeed. "This last deception will be worse than the first," they warned him (Matt. 27:64). Thus the stone was sealed by Pilate's orders and a squad of soldiers assigned to keep watch and prevent anyone from stealing the body and then declaring that a miracle had occurred.

Yet the men whom Jesus had named apostles had no such plan in mind. They were too busy hiding. And certainly, no sorrowing party of women could have overwhelmed a Roman detachment.

The Scandal of the Resurrection

The apostles found it difficult to believe the first story of the Resurrection. And many, not only at that time, but in centuries since, have discounted their story. To them it became a scandalous story.

Some who reject the fact of a bodily Resurrection are willing to allow for something less—a spiritual manifestation, as though the apostles and women with them had seen a ghost! But the New Testament is careful to cover that charge by recounting how Jesus ate with the men at Emmaus and later on the shore of Galilee. (See Luke 24:30 and John 21:12-13). And when Peter was preaching to the household of Cornelius, he said of Jesus: 'They killed Him by hanging Him on a tree, but God raised Him from the dead on the third day and caused Him to be seen. He was not seen by all the people, but by witnesses whom God had already chosen—by us who ate and drank with Him after He rose from the dead" (Acts 10:39-41).

This scandal of the Resurrection is nothing new. Throughout the Book of Acts we read how new believers suffered for their fearless declaration that this man Jesus, who had been certifiably dead and buried—even sealed in a tomb guarded by an elite Roman guard—was now alive! Standing before the Roman provincial governor Felix, Paul declared that the true issue in his trial was the resurrection of the dead (Acts 24:21). A few weeks later, when appearing before King Agrippa, Paul came even nearer to the nub of the unthinkable, as he asked, "Why should any of you consider it incredible that God raises the dead?" (Acts 26:8)

Paul's only response to that question came a few years later, at the edge of a sword on the Appian Way in Rome. There he joined other men and women—threatened, flogged, imprisoned, stoned to death, beheaded, crucified, fed to the lions in the Circus Maximus—willing to endure it all for the alleged folly of their belief in a physical impossibility.

But that was barbaric Rome. In urbane, sophisticated Athens, no one threatened Paul's life when he spoke of the Resurrection. There the reaction was more nearly what one might expect in urbane, sophisticated North America: "When they heard about the resurrection of the dead, some of them sneered" (Acts 17:32). Many scoff today.

For some who call themselves Christians, the phenomenon of the empty tomb is as much an embarrassment to them as it was to the legionnaires responsible to guard it, or to the authorities who had commissioned them. To ease this embarrassment, these professing Christians have accepted inventions trying to account for the missing body, the hundreds of eyewitnesses, and an undeniable commitment to belief that made men and women willing to die for their otherwise ridiculous assertion—that the tomb was empty because Jesus of

Nazareth, the Son of God and Lord of the universe, had conquered death.

Against all other reasoning, naturalistic explanations are offered. The tomb was empty, one line of argument, goes because the Jewish authorities and Roman guards were duped by the oldest con game in the world—"bait and switch." You see, Joseph of Arimathea, Nicodemus, and the rest only pretended to bury Jesus in Joseph's garden tomb. Actually, the body was taken somewhere else. Or, as Ernest Renan and others suggest, the body was there all along, but the magnetism of Jesus' presence lasted beyond His life and made it appear to naive, impressionable women—Mary Magdalene especially—that He was once again alive among them. "Divine power of love!" writes Renan in his *Life of Jesus.* "Sacred moments in which the passion of one possessed gave to the world a resuscitated God!"

But it won't wash. Whatever sophistry one hears from pulpits, whatever scornful intimidating sneer one endures from antisupernaturalists, these feeble attempts at explaining away the Resurrection make fools of their inventors. Today, as 2,000 years ago, the greatest manhunt in history goes on, not for some political revolutionary on the FBI's "Most Wanted" list but for the corpse of a Man who wouldn't stay dead!

The event Christians celebrate at Easter—and should celebrate every day of our lives—is a scandal to the world. It can't be diminished merely to some curious religious aberration. It is nothing less than what it seems: the most preposterous piece of nonsense or the greatest hoax in history—unless it happens to be true!

And because it's true, the miracle of the Resurrection tells us that mankind's age-old dream has also come true, giving every human being an opportunity in Jesus Christ to start over again. The Resurrection brings with it this promise, that because He lives, we too shall live.

6

" . . . He ascended into heaven, and sitteth on the right hand of God the Father Almighty: from thence He shall come to judge the quick and the dead . . ."

In any well-developed story, there must be a series of actions which brings the central character to a climactic moment, to the point of no return, to the brink of some decision after which nothing will again be quite the same. Such action may mark the beginning of a triumphant restoring to order out of the chaos of the past. In the story of the Gospel, the Good News of God's Messenger, that climax occurs at the death, burial, and resurrection of Jesus Christ.

But after the climax must follow the natural sequence of events necessary to an unraveling of the plot. This will fulfill the action and culminate in the central character's return to normal conditions. In many children's tales this part of the story appears as a single anticlimactic line: "And they lived happily ever after."

In the Gospel story, the work of redemption, begun by the birth of Jesus of Nazareth, continued through His ministry, and climaxed by His suffering and resurrection, concludes in three phases. Already past is the Ascension. Going on at present is His intercession on our behalf. Yet to come is the return of Jesus Christ as judge. These are the truths we affirm in this part of the Apostles' Creed.

God's Humiliation

To understand the Ascension and its importance to Christian doctrine, we may need to review the Bible's teaching on the humiliation involved in God's becoming Man. Two beautiful texts in the writings of Paul serve as guides. In his letter to the Philippians, the Apostle is urging his readers to live in unity of love and purpose with each other. To achieve this end, they must learn to practice humility. Paul, wishing to make his injunction concrete and practical, offers them a model—the example of Jesus Himself: "Your attitude should be the same as that of Christ Jesus," he tells them (Phil. 2:5). Then Paul quotes a poem or hymn:

> Who, being in very nature God,
> did not consider equality with God something
> to be grasped,
> but made Himself nothing, taking the very
> nature of a servant,
> being made in human likeness.
> And being found in appearance as a man, He
> humbled Himself
> and became obedient to death—even death on
> a cross! (vv. 6-8)

This is what theologians refer to as the *kenosis*, the "emptying" of God the Son. He demonstrated total willingness to divest Himself of limitless glory and assume the shape and personality of a human being. For the loving purposes of redemption, God the Son laid aside the equality He shared with the Father and the Spirit and became subject to the

Father's will and dependent upon the resources of the Spirit. In other words, He became a man.

Paul's second text illustrates this in the most luminous manner possible, making the unthinkable possible. The world's greatest plutocrat gives away all he possesses to the world's most desperately needy beggar, thereby making the beggar wealthy beyond all comprehension. Paul says, "For you know the grace of our Lord Jesus Christ, that though He was rich, yet for your sakes He became poor, so that you through His poverty might become rich" (2 Cor. 8:9).

The Son's Exaltation

As any reader knows, it's neither fitting nor proper to allow the story to end without restoring the hero to his former state. For example, in the German tale *Lohengrin,* the swan is transformed back into the prince he had been. Similarly, when the great task of redemption had been accomplished, when the Son had been fully obedient to the Father's will, the right consequences followed. Returning to the hymn in Philippians 2, we read;

> Therefore God exalted Him to the highest place and gave Him the name that is above every name, that at the name of Jesus every knee should bow, in heaven and on earth and under the earth, and every tongue confess that Jesus Christ is Lord,

to the glory of God the Father (2:9-11).

The Ascension, however, is something other than the logical return of the Prince to His former condition. It's not merely the resumption of the Son's glorious state through all eternity before Creation, before the Incarnation. "I was by Him, as one brought up with Him: and I was daily His delight, rejoicing always before Him" says the hymn to the preexistent Logos (Prov. 8:30). The Ascension restores the Son to the Father's presence, but not in the same form! Now, for the first time, the realms of divine spirit and sublimity experience the phenomenon of the body—glorified, to be sure, but *a human body* nonetheless!

Scoffers who refuse to believe that Jesus ascended bodily into heaven sometimes argue that the very idea of ascension is primitive; it has no validity in a world in which scientific exploration of space has eliminated the idea of a universe divided into three parts—heaven up there, earth here, and hell down there.

To answer any scoffer by arguing with him is usually an exercise in futility. But it's at least worth pointing out that even our space probes began with an *ascending* rocket—a Saturn or Titan missile which soon traveled out of sight of the viewers at Cape Kennedy, beyond the range of television cameras.

Like the moon-bound rocket, our ascending Lord was also taken up until "a cloud hid Him from their sight" (Acts 1:9).

But is heaven *up there?* We don't know where heaven is. We do know that heaven is *beyond*— beyond this sphere of fleeting time and limited space, beyond human comprehension and imagination. And wherever heaven is, the Lord Jesus Christ is there in His glorified body.

The bodily resurrection of Jesus Christ creates a new order of life. He is the second Adam, the first of a new race of human beings. For, as Paul tells the Corinthians, "Christ has indeed been raised

from the dead, the firstfruits of those who have
fallen asleep. For since death came through a man,
the resurrection of the dead comes also through a
man. For as in Adam all die, so in Christ all will
be made alive. But each in his own turn: Christ,
the firstfruits; then, when He comes, those who
belong to Him" (1 Cor. 15:20-23).

This exaltation of the Son in His incarnate form
is the Father's seal upon the Son's work well done.
The beloved Son, in whom the Father is well-
pleased, receives the Father's benediction in the exalting of His resurrected human form—His hands,
feet, and side still bearing the marks of His suffering. He left the Father's presence to become Man.
As Man, He is welcomed back to be enthroned in
power. Thomas Kelly expresses our wonder in his
hymn:

> Look, ye saints, the sight is glorious;
> See the Man of Sorrows now;
> From the fight returned victorious,
> Every knee to Him shall bow:
> Crown Him! crown Him!
> Crowns become the Victor's brow.

A Fulfillment of Prophecy

The ascension or exaltation of Jesus Christ also
fulfills repeated prophecies, particularly in the
Psalms. One of the most familiar is "Lift up your
heads, O ye gates; and be ye lifted up, ye everlasting doors; and the King of glory shall come in. Who
is this King of glory? The Lord strong and mighty,
the Lord mighty in battle. . . . Who is this King of
glory? The Lord of hosts, He is the King of glory"
(Ps. 24:7-8,10). In Psalm 68, the writer envisions
the ascended Lord's triumphant return: "The char-

iots of God are twenty thousand, even thousands of angels: the Lord is among them, as in Sinai, in the holy place. Thou hast ascended on high, Thou hast led captivity captive: Thou hast received gifts for men" (vv. 17-18).

Perhaps the most important prophecy in this connection is found in Psalm 110. It speaks not only of the Ascension but also of the place of authority and power now invested in the Lord Jesus Christ as mediator and advocate. "The Lord said unto my Lord, Sit Thou at My right hand, until I make Thine enemies Thy footstool. The Lord shall send the rod of Thy strength out of Zion: rule Thou in the midst of Thine enemies. Thy people shall be willing in the day of Thy power, in the beauties of holiness from the womb of the morning: Thou hast the dew of Thy youth. The Lord hath sworn, and will not repent, Thou art a priest forever after the order of Melchizedek. The Lord at Thy right hand shall strike through kings in the day of His wrath" (vv. 1-5). This Psalm is quoted many times in the New Testament—three times in the synoptic Gospels, when Jesus wished to assert His Lordship (see Matt. 22:41-45; Mark 12:35-37; and Luke 20:41-44). In Peter's Pentecost sermon, he used this text as his clinching point: "Exalted to the right hand of God, He has received from the Father the promised Holy Spirit, and has poured out what you now see and hear. For David did not ascend to heaven, and yet he said, 'The Lord said to My Lord: Sit at My right hand until I make Your enemies Your footstool'" (Acts 2:33-35).

Finally, throughout the letter to the Hebrews, in which the writer uses the model of the high priest and his rituals, Psalm 110 receives prominence. The argument is complex and needs to be studied in its full context; here we can only summarize.

Jesus Christ is both the Lamb of God and the great High Priest. He originates the priestly succession of Melchizedek (see Gen. 14:18-20). Thereby He transcends the natural line of priests, the sons of Levi, establishing a new code of law based not upon the threat of death but upon "the power of an indestructible life" (Heb. 7:16). Like that mysterious Melchizedek, king of Salem and priest of God (see Heb. 7:1-10), the Son of God has no beginning and no end. So, "because Jesus lives forever, he has a permanent priesthood" (Heb. 7:24).

As our High Priest or representative at the right hand of God the Father, Jesus Christ's specific mission is "to save completely those who come to God through Him"; to this end, "He always lives to intercede for them" (Heb. 7:25). He is to be our defense attorney, interceding for us when Satan the accuser (see Rev. 12:10) brings his charges.

The Meaning of the Incarnation and Ascension

Now, perhaps, we begin to understand the importance of the Incarnation and the glorified body in which Jesus Christ intercedes for us. That body is a reminder to the Father that the Son Himself was once one of us. He, like us, was "made a little lower than the angels" (Ps. 8:5). But now, the author of the letter to the Hebrews tells us, we see Jesus "crowned with glory and honor because He suffered death, so that by the grace of God He might taste death for everyone" (Heb. 2:9). Furthermore, His Incarnation means that we enjoy a special relationship with God the Son as our Mediator and Advocate: "For we do not have a high priest who is unable to sympathize with our weaknesses, but we have one who has been tempted in every way, just as we are—yet was without sin." (Heb. 4:15).

We are made confident to believe that our sins are forgiven as the Father accepts the Son's death for us. It is enough. Through Him our debt is paid; our sins are forgotten. With such assurance, we are free to enjoy this encouragement: "Let us then approach the throne of grace with confidence, so that we may receive mercy and find grace to help us in our time of need (Heb. 4:16).

Jesus' Return

The Creed declares that Jesus Christ is the ascended Lord and our "advocate with the Father" (1 John 2:1, KJV). Then the Creed goes on to say, ". . . from thence He shall come to judge the quick and the dead." In the fullest account of the Ascension (see Acts 1:1-11), Luke tells Theophilus of an angelic message to the bewildered apostles: "They were looking intently up into the sky as He was going, when suddenly two men dressed in white stood beside them. 'Men of Galilee,' they said, 'why do you stand here looking into the sky? This same Jesus, who has been taken from you into heaven, will come back in the same way you have seen Him go into heaven'" (Acts 1:10-11). This *same* Jesus— the resurrected and ascended Lord—will come back *in the same way!* His bodily resurrection and bodily ascension determine a similar bodily return. Not, however, this time as a helpless infant, but as the reigning Lord of all the worlds, the one whom Abraham recognized as "Judge of all the earth" (Gen. 18:25).

Neither the Creed nor the Bible tells us exactly *when* the Lord Jesus Christ will return. Nor should we presume to speculate, since Jesus Himself said, "No one knows about that day or hour, not even the angels in heaven, nor the Son, but only the Father" (Matt. 24:36). Yet, while we must not indulge in guessing games or follow after profiteering prophets, we're cautioned to be constantly on watch for "the signs of the times" (Matt. 16:3; see also Matt. 25:13). These signs are listed in Matthew 24:4-32, followed by severe warnings throughout Matthew 25.

Since history has scarcely known a period free from wars and rumors of wars, or famines and earthquakes, we do well to avoid citing any specific conflict or natural disaster as conclusive evidence by which to date the return of Jesus Christ. However, of this much we may be sure: The timing of the Lord's return depends upon one condition still remaining to be fulfilled, namely the witness of the Gospel throughout the world. Jesus said, "And this Gospel of the kingdom will be preached in the whole world as a testimony to all nations, and then the end will come" (Matt. 24:14).

One more word of caution, lest we be like the foolish virgins who let their lamps go out (see Matt. 25:1-12). We must be ready for the return of Jesus Christ at all times; otherwise, He warns us, "the Son of Man will come at an hour when you do not expect Him" (Matt. 24:44; see also 1 Thes. 5:1-11).

The Reason for Jesus' Return
The Creed does not say anything about the manner of the Lord's return. To discover *how* He will come,

we must study such passages as 1 Corinthians 15: 51-55, 1 Thessalonians 4:13-18, and Revelation 4— 22. But the Creed is quite clear about *why* Jesus Christ is coming again: "He shall come to *judge*."

In preaching to the Roman centurion Cornelius, Peter told him and his household about Jesus of Nazareth, His life, death, and resurrection. Then Peter said, "He commanded us to preach to the people and to testify that He is the one whom God appointed as Judge of the living and the dead. All the prophets testify about Him that everyone who believes in Him receives forgiveness of sins through His name" (Acts 10:42-43).

In Athens, the Court of Areopagus met on the outcropping just below the Parthenon and other famous temples of the Acropolis. At this site were tried some of Athens' most notorious criminals— murderers mostly. But on a certain day, the Apostle Paul tried another case. He argued on behalf of God the Father Almighty, Maker of heaven and earth, against pagan idolatry and ignorance. As he reached his conclusion, Paul declared God's mercy for past offences but warned about the present and the future: "In the past God overlooked such ignorance, but now He commands all people everywhere to repent. For He has set a day when He will judge the world with justice by the Man He has appointed. He has given proof of this to all men by raising Him from the dead" (Acts 17:30-31).

These texts make plain the apostle's teaching. Jesus Christ's authority as Lord gives Him authority to judge the Creation, both living and dead, over which He rules. In England, a judge's robe and wig symbolize his legal authority. Jesus Christ needs no such tokens; His conquest over death is its own badge of authority. He is the one "designated by God . . . a Man of His choosing," as Peter and Paul tell us. By His Resurrection power, Jesus Christ is Lord and Judge of all creatures (see Rom. 14:9). He supersedes the limits of time and death, calling before His court both the living and the dead to be judged by His criteria.

Beneath the looming heights of Mount Parnassus at Delphi in Greece is one of the oldest athletic stadiums. The site may date from 582 B.C., when the Pythian Games were reorganized to be held midway between each Olympiad. This stadium is a narrow horseshoe, some 200 yards long. There the standard events were conducted—running, jumping, throwing, and wrestling. Rows of stone bleachers ring the track. Exactly in the middle of the stadium, facing the wrestling pit, is a special bench remarkably well-preserved after the centuries. It's the seat set apart for the judges who awarded, at Delphi, the laurel wreath or garland to all victors who had competed according to the rules.

In writing his last letter from prison, Paul employed the metaphor of a classical athlete in these ancient games: "I have finished the race, I have kept the faith. Now there is in store for me the crown of righteousness, which the Lord, the righteous Judge, will award to me on that day—and not only to me, but also to all who have longed for His appearing" (2 Tim. 4:7-8).

For the athlete at Delphi, keeping faith with the rules was the only way to win the coveted prize. For us, the only way to receive "the garland of righteousness" from "the all-just Judge" is to keep faith with His rules—which means that we must "throw off everything that hinders and the sin that so easily entangles, and let us run with perseverance the race marked out for us. Let us fix our eyes on Jesus, the Pioneer and Perfector of our faith, who for the joy set before Him endured the cross, scorning its shame, and sat down at the right hand of the throne of God" (Heb. 12:1-2).

7

"... I Believe in the Holy Ghost ..."

At first glance, it seems strange that the Apostles' Creed declares nothing more than this about the Holy Spirit. Because its clause is so terse and abbreviated, some theologians regard the Apostles' Creed as deficient in its treatment of the doctrine of the Holy Spirit. Some even suggest that, unlike the so-called Nicene Creed (which devotes more than six times the number of words to the Holy Spirit), the Apostles' Creed is actually slighting to the Holy Spirit. Others even go so far as to say that the Apostles' Creed is non-Trinitarian.

But to argue this way is to misread the Apostles' Creed. Each of its three paragraphs specifies the work of one member of the Trinity. In the first two paragraphs, God the Father wills and ordains Creation; God the Son, by His incarnation and exaltation, redeems that fallen Creation. In the final paragraph, God the Holy Spirit sanctifies the Church and brings its members into fellowship, assuring them of their sins' forgiveness and the promise of life everlasting.

Of course, there's no ignoring the fact that the

creed commonly known as Nicene is more explicit and expansive in dealing with the subject of the Holy Spirit. It reads: "And I believe in the Holy Ghost, the Lord and Giver of life, who proceedeth from the Father and the Son; who with the Father and the Son together is worshipped and glorified; who spake by the prophets." Yet even this statement, with all its unquestioned beauty, clarity, and truth, can't be considered a complete expression of the full teaching of the Bible on the Holy Spirit. It only amplifies what the Apostles' Creed also declares—that is, belief *in* the Holy Spirit.

The important thing, it seems to me, is not how little or much the Creed says, but how much it implies. Certainly the Apostles' Creed is open to the teaching of Scripture regarding the Holy Spirit. Essentially that teaching begins with a recognition that the Spirit shares with the Father and the Son divine Personhood and equality. Or, to say it in slightly different terms, like the Father and Son, the Spirit is a unique Person, wholly divine and wholly equal with the two other members of the Trinity.

The Breath of God

What are the unique attributes of the Holy Ghost or Holy Spirit? First, it's worth remembering that our word *ghost* comes from an Old English word closely related to the German *geist,* meaning spirit. So ghost and spirit are synonyms. *Spirit,* in turn, comes to us from the Latin word *spiritus,* meaning breath or wind. From this word we obtain our various terms for breathing: respiratory, inspiration, expire. The Greek word is *pneuma,* from which we derive such words as pneumatic and pneumonia.

Therefore, etymologically speaking, the Holy Spirit is the Breath of God.

The Breath of God animates Creation by His presence. In Genesis, the first gesture indicating the Father's will to create is the moving of the Spirit; the very Wind or Breath of God, "moved upon the face of the waters" (Gen. 1:2).

The Holy Spirit is also the source of that eternal breath possessed solely by human beings, setting us apart from every other creature. We read that "the Lord God formed man of the dust of the ground, and breathed into his nostrils the breath of life; and the man became a living soul" (Gen. 2:7).

The Holy Spirit is "the Lord and Giver of Life," as the Nicene Creed declares. The English poet John Dryden translated a ninth century hymn, "Veni Creator Spiritus,"

> Creator Spirit, by whose aid
> The world's foundations first were laid,
> Come, visit every humble mind;
> Come, pour Thy joys on human kind;
> From sin and sorrow set us free,
> And make Thy temples worthy Thee.

This ought to be answer enough to the question, "Why is life sacred?" All life, whether human, animal, or vegetable, is the immediate and present product of the Trinity's creative powers. In a disarming and whimsical book called *The Third Peacock*, Robert F. Capon describes on-going Creation this way:

> What happens is not that the Trinity manufactures the first duck and then the ducks take over the duck business as a kind of cottage industry. It is that every duck, down at the

roots of its being, at the level where what is needed is not the ability to fertilize duck eggs, but the moxie to stand outside of nothing—to *be* when there is no necessity of being—every duck, at that level, is a response to the creative act of God. In terms of the analogy, it means that God the Father *thinks up* duck #47,307 for the month of May, A.D. 1970, that God the Spirit rushes over to the edge of the formless void and, with unutterable groanings, *broods* duck #47,307, and that over His brooding God the Son, the eternal Word, triumphantly *shouts*, "Duck #47,307!" And presto! You have a duck. Not one, you will note, tossed off in response to some mindless decree that there might as well be ducks as alligators, but one neatly fielded up in a game of delight by the eternal archetypes of Tinker, Evers and Chance.

"The world," Capon concludes, "is not God's surplus inventory of artifacts; it is a whole barrelful of the apples of His eye, constantly juggled, relished and exchanged by the persons of the Trinity. No wonder we love circuses, games and magic; they prove we are in the image of God." [1]

The Divine Light and Life

The Greek word for *light* used in the New Testament is *phōs,* meaning radiance, from which we take our word *photograph.* At Creation, the Father willed, the Son spoke, the Spirit illumined. It's important to note that, all through the account of Creation in Genesis 1, the narrator tells us that God

---

[1] Robert F. Capon, *The Third Peacock* (New York: Doubleday and Company, 1971), pp. 13-14.

commanded, then *made* to suit His command, the vault of the sky, the seas and dry land, astral lights, and countless living things. All these God *made* in His act of Creation. However, His first command was not creative but illuming. "Let there be light" was God's summons for the Spirit to exercise His divine attribute already evident, forever shining throughout eternity as the radiance of God. The Light of the Holy Spirit was called upon to enlighten the cosmos being brought into existence.

So the Light of Creation is the very Life of God. John tells us: "In Him was life, and that life was the light of men" (John 1:4). It's the light supernal and supreme over every power of darkness (see John 1:5). It's also the universal light, "the true light that gives light to every man" (John 1:9). Perhaps the Apostle refers to what we call "the light of conscience." If so, then conscience is part of the image of God in which we've been made (see Gen. 1:26-27). In any case, the Holy Spirit is responsible for this common gift of grace upon all human beings.

As the Spirit brings life, I'm convinced that an important evidence of the Holy Spirit at work is our concern to sustain life through health and medical services. In North America and Europe, where the Christian message has pervaded our history for centuries, we take medical care for granted. But in many parts of the world, where the light of the Gospel shines only dimly, medical care is scarce.

On a trip through Asia, one is astonished by the official lack of concern for people. Many die in the streets. In Bangladesh and India, marketplaces swarm with destitute, diseased, and crippled beggars. For the most part they are ignored because, the pagan religion teaches, their *karma* or fate destined by the gods must not be interfered with. In most of Asia there is no medicare, no emergency room, no ambulance service, no available hospital, no healing arts for the common people—except where a Christian mission hospital stands. Without the Christian hospital at Malumghat, Bangladesh for instance, thousands in the surrounding region would die without diagnosis or care.

The Holy Spirit compels us to obey the command of Jesus Christ: "Heal the sick" (Matt. 10:8).

Our Re-creation

In the same way that the Holy Spirit participated in the original Creation, so the Holy Spirit is also responsible for our re-creation, our rebirth through faith as children of God. He breathes, He enlightens. He is the *pneuma* who fills our beings with the Breath of Life. He is the *phōs* of whom Paul spoke: "For God who said, 'Let light shine out of darkness,' made His light shine in our hearts to give us the light of the knowledge of the glory of God in the face of Christ" (2 Cor. 4:6).

When we believe in God and in Jesus Christ His only Son our Lord, we're given new life. The presence of the Holy Spirit is God's assurance to us that we have become His children, His heirs. Jesus Himself promised, "I am the Light of the world. Whoever follows Me will never walk in darkness, but will have the light of life" (John 8:12). Because Jesus of Nazareth embodied the fullness of God (see Col. 2:9)—including the will of the Father and the word of the Son—He could claim the light of the Spirit and offer that light to all who believed in Him. In confidence, therefore, we can utter that beautiful evening prayer: "Lighten our darkness, we beseech Thee, O Lord; and by Thy great mercy defend us from all perils and dangers of this night; for the love of Thy only Son, our Saviour, Jesus Christ. Amen."

The Divine Inspirator and Revealer

The Holy Spirit has still another responsibility derived from His attributes of Breath and Light. He is to *inspire* and *reveal*. He inspires us to do the will of God. He reveals to us specifically what that will may be. He inspired the written Word and now reveals its truth. He inspires us with His gifts of grace, revealing how best to use those gifts in Christ's service. This has always been the responsibility of the Spirit. Prompted by the Father, given verbal expression by the Son, "men spoke from God as they were carried along by the Holy Spirit" (2 Peter 1:21).

This threefold working of God through His servants shows itself in instance after instance. In Moses' case, the will of God and the Word expressed themselves in flames—the product of Breath and Light (see Ex. 3:1-15). Isaiah saw the radiance of God's glory, heard the divine utterances of God's holiness and judgment, felt the cleansing fire searing away his sins, and knew his mission (see Isa. 6:1-13). At Jesus' transfiguration, once more the unity of the Godhead showed itself in will, Word, and light: the command of the Father, the presence of the Word, the sublime light of the Spirit (see Luke 9:28-36).

The same experience marked the conversion of Saul of Tarsus on his way to Damascus. He was compelled by the Father, addressed by the Son, dazzled blind by the Spirit (see Acts 9:1-22). And while imprisoned on Patmos, John too knew the presence of divine volition, expression, and illumination—God the Father, God the Son, and God the Holy Spirit (see Rev. 1:9-19).

It's clear from each of these examples that the Holy Spirit's work includes impelling men and women of God to minister the Good News. Moses didn't remain a shepherd over Jethro's flock. Jesus didn't permit Peter and the other two disciples to build their spiritual ivory towers on the mountain top. And at the base of our mountains await those whose needs can only be satisfied by the power of Jesus Christ and the Holy Spirit working through us. Lacking the transcendent vision of the glorified Christ and the power His Spirit gives, we are as futile as the companions of Jesus who could not heal the afflicted child (see Luke 9:37-43). But we are equally powerless to help if we remain isolated on the mountain of some spiritual retreat. As Frank Mason North says in his grand hymn, we need to be found at the crossroads of life, "where sound the cries of race and clan . . . In haunts of wretchedness and needs, on shadowed thresholds dark with fears." Our prayer ought to be,

O Master, from the mountain side
Make haste to heal these hearts of pain;
Among these restless throngs abide,
O tread the city's streets again.

Then we must be willing to follow where the Spirit leads us.

The Gifts of the Spirit

No discussion of the Holy Spirit can be complete without reference to the gifts of the Spirit as they are presented in the New Testament. The Greek word for gift is *charisma,* from which we obtain both the popular description, as in "He has a great deal of charisma with his audience," and the religious description, as in "charismatic movement." Both words suggest giftedness; the second, specifically endowed with divine gifts.

Now, according to Paul's first letter to the Corinthians, spiritual gifts are many in number. These gifts appear to have a hierarchy or priority of value, although no gift is to be disdained because each contributes its part to making up what Paul describes as the Body of Christ (see 1 Cor. 12:12-31). What that hierarchy is, we may discover in a moment.

The first gift, the fundamental necessity, is the gift of sanctified vision. Through this "holy sight" the Holy Spirit reveals to us who Jesus is. "No one can say, 'Jesus is Lord,' except," says Paul, "by the Holy Spirit" (1 Cor. 12:3). For the Christian, everything starts with this gift of revelation. No one who's confused or the least bit uncertain about the Lordship of Jesus Christ can make legitimate claim to possessing any of the other gifts of the Holy Spirit.

But once we have received the revelation of truth concerning who Jesus is, we're open to receive even more from God. "There are different kinds of spiritual gifts but the same Spirit. There are different kinds of service, but the same Lord" (1 Cor. 12:4-5). Notice the repeated plural: *kinds,* not a kind. What does this mean?

I happen to own a car manufactured by the Ford Motor Company—which tells you very little because Ford makes several kinds of automobiles:

subcompacts, compacts, intermediates, full-sized. Even within the single type of car there may be many different models—two-door, four-door, hard-top, station wagon, and the rest. Together these kinds comprise the Ford line of cars.

I hope this analogy suggests that, in addition to the Spirit's many different gifts, each individual gift may take on any of several different appearances, forms, shapes, modes, and means of service. This means that the gifts enumerated by Paul—wise speech, putting the deepest thoughts into plain language, the gifts of faith, healing and other miraculous powers, prophecy, the discernment of true from false, ecstatic utterance or interpretation (see 1 Cor. 12:8-10)—are manifestly different in each individual.

No two speakers, for example, ought to speak alike. "The gift of wise speech" is channeled through an individual personality. His public oration grows out of the character and style that mark the speaker's unique use of his gift. So too with the ability to "speak with knowledge" (1 Cor. 12:8), or any of the other gifts. Each is, first of all, the property of the Holy Spirit to distribute as He wishes to whomever He wishes. Thereafter, the Spirit expects each individual to use his gift according to the maturity, experience, and grace granted him by the Holy Spirit Himself.

We're expressly forbidden to covet someone else's gift. We're to think of ourselves as belonging to a body, a corporate entity, in which we function organically, each part benefiting the whole. Paul uses various limbs and organs to illustrate his point. In essence, what he means is this: "Suppose the person with the gift of faith should say, 'Because I don't speak in strange tongues, I don't belong to the Body of Christ.' That person does belong nonetheless. Suppose the person with the gift of explaining difficult doctrines should say, 'Because I don't have the gift of healing, I don't belong to the Body of Christ.' That person does still belong to the Body" (see 1 Cor. 12:14-16).

How strange, with teaching so clear, that so many earnest Christians are troubled with inferiority complexes because other Christians disparage one gift while exalting another! How ironic that the one gift most often elevated, the so-called gift of tongues, should be the one Paul treats as least important! For Paul writes specifically to the point: "In the Church God has appointed first of all apostles, second prophets, third teachers, then workers of miracles, also those having gifts of healing, those able to help others, those with gifts of administration, and finally those speaking in different kinds of tongues" (1 Cor. 12:28).

The order prescribed is clear: first of all, apostles; second, prophets; third, teachers; and then the list that follows. Furthermore, since the gift of apostleship had apparently been foreclosed by the choice of Jesus Christ Himself, the highest ambition in service the Corinthians might strive for wasn't speaking in tongues or interpreting or working miracles, but the act of prophesying. The word in Greek sometimes refers to foretelling the future, but its primary meaning is more closely related to a forceful and effective manner of teaching—in other words, what we would honor today as the divine gift of expository preaching.

But surely, Paul himself must have recognized the probable hazards in classifying one gift over another. That's why, right in the middle of his discussion of the charismatic blessings from the Holy Spirit, he threw in a parenthesis perhaps more important than his major point—the great poem on love! (1 Cor. 13)

Every Christian has been united in Jesus Christ. As branches to the True Vine, we are nourished and cared for so that we might "bear much fruit" (John 15:8). That fruit of which Jesus speaks is described by Paul as "love, joy, peace, patience, kindness, goodness, faithfulness, gentleness and self-control" (Gal. 5:22-23). These are the fruit of the Spirit which, unlike the Spirit's gifts, ought to be openly demonstrated in all our lives.

The doctrine of the Holy Spirit is a demanding study. Jesus Himself waited until the last possible opportunity before beginning to instruct His disciples. Even then, they were ignorant until the Spirit quickened them and revealed Himself to them. So too shall we be, until we experience the answer to our prayer:

> Spirit of God, descend upon my heart;
> Wean it from earth, through all its pulses move;
> Stoop to my weakness, mighty as Thou art,
> And make me love Thee as I ought to love.

8

"... *The Holy Catholic Church* ..."

A friend's son, playing with a neighbor child, asked his playmate, "What church do you go to?"

"I'm a Catholic. What are you?"

Johnny hesitated for a moment, thinking over the question. He and his family attended a fellowship that met each week in the home of a man named Horace Klenk.

"I'm a Klenk," Johnny answered proudly. His little friend simply nodded and accepted the designation. If it was good enough for Johnny, it was good enough for him.

"I believe in . . . the Holy Catholic Church," says the Apostles' Creed. When most of us use or hear the word "church," we're often much like the two little boys in our thinking. "Church" has come to mean, almost exclusively, an architectural structure to which we go on certain occasions to engage in what are called "religious services." Usually the building itself has characteristics to indicate the kinds of activities carried on within it. A Gothic cathedral may well have rows of wooden pews facing a draped altar on which stands a golden cross. Or a former supermarket may now have theatre seats facing a plain communion table or a pulpit. In either case, however, what draws us to designate the building as a "church" is something other than its physical makeup. It has to do with the fact that to this structure persons in our community come togeher for an experience called "worship." If we find it with them in this building, we soon begin to speak possessively of "our church."

In many instances, "our church" is corporately and perhaps legally connected with a national association of churches. This larger organization obtains its unity from a shared emphasis upon one or more doctrines, such as a particular view of the timing and nature of water baptism; a particular understanding of the congregation's right to govern itself; a particular opinion of the role of elders or bishops in governing "our church." From this sense of unity the larger body takes its name, its *denomination,* as Baptist, Congregational, Presbyterian, Episcopal, etc. "Our church" aligns itself as a member of that denomination. Or perhaps "our church" remains independent of any ties to a formal organization, even though we share many of the same beliefs.

What I've been describing is the way most people describe "our church," at least in North America. The corporate body known as the "church" is fragmented into some 600 denominations and sects. Some denominations exist today long after their initial cause for forming has been forgotten. Other groups remain as monuments to the egos of their founders. In spite of the fact that we may sing, "We are not divided, All one body we," honesty would compel us to confess that the ideal is far from the reality. All too often "our church" bears little resemblance to what Jesus Christ called "My Church" (Matt. 16:18).

The Original Church

The Church that Jesus Christ founded was an extension of the original fellowship established by God's covenants with those who chose to follow him—Abel, Enoch, Noah, Abraham, Isaac, Jacob, Moses, and the Israelites at Sinai, the faithful remnant of exiles who listened to and heeded the Book of the Law read to them by Ezra, and others. In other words, the idea of the Church goes back to the Old Testament idea of a "chosen people," called out by God to worship Him and serve Him throughout the world. The Greek and Latin words we translate as church are similar: *ekklesia* or *ecclesia*, from which we get ecclesiastical. The original word means "an assembly or congregation of citizens." This word was used in the Septuagint version of the Old Testament, translated in the second century B.C., to speak of the Israelites' assembly (see Deut. 9:10, 10:4, 18:16).

We can gain some clearer sense of this historic relationship between the Church of Jesus Christ and the Old Testament's people of God from reading a passage in Peter's first letter: "As you come to Him, the living Stone—rejected by men but chosen by God and precious to Him—you also, like living stones, are being built into a spiritual house to be a holy priesthood, offering spiritual sacrifices acceptable to God through Jesus Christ" (1 Peter 2:4-5).

Peter was obviously relying on his readers' imagination in constructing a metaphorical temple, of which Jesus Christ is the cornerstone, His followers the building blocks. Then Peter changed his figure of speech: from stones forming an edifice to priests offering sacrifices. Peter's Jewish readers would know that to be a priest, one had to be born into the nation of Israel and into the family of Levi. This particular theme—our special designation by God—Peter takes up in the next paragraph.

After he has condemned those who have no faith, who stumble over the fact that Jesus is both Messiah and Lord, Peter writes: "But you are a chosen people, a royal priesthood, a holy nation, a people belonging to God, that you may declare the praise of Him who called you out of darkness into His wonderful light. Once you were not a people, but now you are the people of God; once you had not received mercy, but now you have received mercy" (1 Peter 2:9-10).

This is the Church Peter knew, from that day at Caesarea Philippi, when Jesus Christ responded to Peter's confession and promised to build His church, and from that day in Jerusalem, when the Holy Spirit filled the group of Jesus' followers and caused them to spill over in eagerness and ecstasy. The Church is the people of God who, by faith in Jesus Christ, have been given the immediate blessing of the Holy Spirit's presence to assure us of our relationship with the Father through the Son.

Though some who slight the Church would call it merely one of man's institutions, the Church is ordained by God the Father, founded by God the Son, and cared for by God the Holy Spirit. The Church is the Spirit's particular concern. It's His work to mold and fashion the Church, from a nucleus of 120 believers huddled together in Jerusalem into today's transnational, transcultural assembly of people whose love for God shows itself in their love for others.

Proclamation

The purpose of the Church is both proclamation and edification. Jesus' final words to His disciples in Galilee, just before His ascension, are called the Great Commission. He commissioned His followers to speak in His name and with His authority: "All authority in heaven and earth has been given to Me. Therefore go and make disciples of all nations, baptizing them in the name of the Father and of the Son and of the Holy Spirit, and teaching them to obey everything that I have commanded you. And surely I will be with you always, to the very end of the age" (Matt. 28:18-20). The Church is to serve as a voice for God, as evangelists or bearers of the Good News, making known God's claims upon the human race and all Creation through the grace of His Son and gifts of His Spirit.

But the Church is required to do more than merely broadcast the Good News. Evangelizing is more than announcing. Jesus Christ calls His Church to "make disciples of all nations"—literally, to place someone under the discipline of learning, the way a coach teaches an athlete a difficult feat of skill. Itinerant evangelists can scarcely accomplish this work of discipleship. Nothing in the New Testament suggests any pattern of haste and superficiality, but rather an emphasis on nurturing those who have been saved.

The mark of effective evangelism will be the baptism of those who receive the Good News and accept the authority of God the Father, Son, and Holy Spirit, as conveyed through the Church. The fact that baptism is specified in the names of the Trinity shows that the Church operates under the blessing and sanction of the Godhead.

Edification

Proclamation may have rapid, almost instantaneous results, as happened when Philip preached to the Ethiopian (Acts 8:26-40). Edification—the building up of one's spiritual character—requires continual experience and growth. The means of edification comes through the Church's ministry of teaching. The content of that teaching has been clearly outlined by the Lord Jesus Christ Himself— "Teaching them to obey everything I have commanded you." The Church's curriculum should consist of instruction in obedience to Jesus Christ's commandments given to His apostles.

Obedience has become an unpopular word in our generation. But the Church has no alternative to offer. We can't simply *recommend* it might be a good idea if we loved one another. We can only instruct each other in the commandment given by Jesus (see John 15:10-17). We can't set up a system of collective bargaining to settle personal differences; we can only follow the commandment given by our Lord (see Matt. 18:15-17).

The Church is further obligated to teach obedience to *everything* Jesus Christ commands. Accepting the power of the Holy Spirit to inspire and reveal truth to the apostles, we believe that Jesus Christ speaks through the epistles as well as through the four Gospels. We can't rummage through the New Testament, discarding one book and accepting another. Unless Scripture so exempts us, we are under its warrant and must obey.

"This is love for God," wrote the Apostle John, "to obey His commands. And His commands are not burdensome" (1 John 5:3). How true! In His service we have perfect freedom! And to encourage us in obedience, we have the assurance of Jesus Christ's divine presence, in the Person of the Holy Spirit, "to the very end of the age."

The Structure of the Church

What about the structure of the Church? Several metaphors appear throughout the New Testament. Some we've already glanced at: the temple whose cornerstone is Jesus Christ; the royal priesthood whose High Priest is Jesus Christ; the Body whose Head is Jesus Christ; the Bride whose Bridegroom is Jesus Christ. These leave no doubt as to whom the Church is responsible. We are "the sheep of His pasture" (Ps. 100:3); He is "that great Shepherd of the sheep" (Heb. 13:20, KJV).

Jesus Christ laid down no rules for governing His Church. But by the very nature of God's dealings with humanity through the Jewish nation—and the fact that the Incarnation occurred among the Jews—it's not surprising that the first Christians should adapt some of their Jewish traditions and customs to useful service in the Church. Certainly, the Acts of the Apostles shows us how attached these early believers remained to Jewish practices. Among these were the custom of formal meetings for common worship, the study of the Law and the Prophets, and the election of elders. The Greek word for elder is *presbyteros,* from which the Presbyterian denomination takes its name.

The Early Church also undertook to meet its needs by launching out on its own innovations. Jesus Christ had appointed the Twelve Apostles. When one of them defaulted, the rest voted for a replacement (see Acts 1:15-26). Later, in a crisis over the delegation of responsibilities, the Church instituted the office of deacon. The Greek word *diakonos* simply means "servant" (see Acts 6:1-6).

Soon, however, persecution forced the Church to disperse from Jerusalem. In some instances, an apostle accompanied the refugees. Where no apostle was present, we're left to assume that some Christian felt himself summoned by God to take leadership. But such a person was never called an apostle; these men became known as shepherds. Interestingly, the Latin word for shepherd is well known to us as *pastor*. In addressing the elders of the Ephesian church, Paul refers to their role as shepherds when he speaks of "the flock of which the Holy Spirit has made you overseers. Be shepherds of the Church of God" (Acts 20:28). Then he warns against "savage wolves" who "will not spare the flock" (20:29).

One other term appears in this same passage: "overseers," the Greek word *episkopoi,* from which the Episcopal church receives both its name and model in Scripture. Other uses of the word or its derivatives appear in Philippians 1:1, 1 Timothy 3:2, and Titus 1:7.

But whatever the government in the New Testament Church (and there are many persons of conviction who differ on this matter) one thing was clear: no Christian was to go it alone. No individualism was to replace the corporate unity of believers as members of the Body of Christ. Not

Peter, nor Paul, nor any of the apostles was a law unto himself. Each was answerable to the Church wherever it was constituted (see Acts 15:1-35; Gal. 1:11—2:16).

Why was this so? Why were strong-willed men like Peter and Paul subordinate to the Church and its elders? (see Acts 21:18-26) Because it is the *Holy* Church, instituted by God.

Worship
God has always presented Himself to human beings as a God of holiness. It is His foremost attribute. His holiness is His guarantee of truth. His worship must be offered in holiness (see Ex. 15:11; Ps. 89:35; 1 Chron. 16:29). Places He chooses to reveal Himself are always recognizably holy: Bethel, the burning bush in the desert, Mount Sinai, the Tabernacle, the Temple on Mount Zion.

In Christianity's earliest years, the Church had no such worship center as the magnificent Temple at Jerusalem. Instead, the Church met in homes (see Rom. 16:5, 1 Cor. 16:19, Col. 4:15, Phile. 2), in open places (see Acts 16:11-15), and eventually even in the underground tombs in Rome called catacombs. Still, each Christian possessed a sense of sanctity in worship, wherever it was held, because as Paul exclaimed in a question to the Corinthians, "Don't you know that you yourselves are God's temple, and that God's Spirit lives in you?" (1 Cor. 3:16)

The Holy Spirit in the life of every believer constructs a Temple holy to the Lord—the human body itself—a symbol of that greater Body which is the Church and of which Jesus Christ is Head. If so, aren't our bodies too sacred for us to allow them to be defiled and polluted by the ravages of corruption and sin?

Now that we have the liberty to erect places of worship, we need to guard against either of two errors. First, we cannot fix God in a permanent location because the Holy of Holies is within us. We must not become shrine worshipers, obsessed with the thought of God's presence in *this* place and nowhere else.

The 1956 Olympic 400-meters champion, Charles Jenkins, was asked about praying during a race. "On the backstretch I always start feeling tired, so I just ask the Lord, 'O God, you pick up my legs, and I'll lay 'em down!' " For a Christian, the Church is in the arena as well as in the sanctuary.

We must also avoid too casual an attitude toward corporate worship. Everything, beginning with the organist's prelude, should be designed to direct our thinking toward God. Little things often interrupt our thoughts about God, and distractions of various kinds rob our fragile concentration. Informality that detracts from reverential awe becomes a hindrance to worship. And one might wonder why a congregation bothers to spend considerable money for a sanctuary if the people fail to take advantage of the inspiration it is designed to produce.

The sanctuary is meaningful to us and requires our reverence because in its confines many of the holiest moments of our lives are enacted—our baptism, our partaking of bread and wine, our marriage, the consecration of our children to the Lord, the dedication of lives in holy ordination to serve Jesus Christ, our weekly fellowship. Whether "our church" happens to be a chapel or a cathedral, we must honor it as a spot where God meets us, saying as Jacob did at Bethel, "This is none other but the house of God, and this is the gate of heaven" (Gen. 28:17).

The "Catholic" Church

The word "catholic" troubles only those who don't know that the word means "universal." When the Apostles' Creed speaks of the Holy Catholic Church it extends the Church's scope to its fullest dimensions. There's nothing either provincial or national about the Church of Jesus Christ. His commandment to the Apostles shows His intention: "You will be My witnesses in Jerusalem, and in all Judea and Samaria, and to the ends of the earth" (Acts 1:8).

Ignatius, the Bishop of Antioch who died in A.D. 107, said, "Wherever Christ Jesus is, there is the Catholic Church." In A.D. 250, when the martyr Pionius was on trial at Smyrna, his judges asked him what he was called. "A Christian," he replied. "To what church do you belong?" "To the Catholic Church," he answered.

The rapid expansion of the Church to become the Catholic Church is a thrilling story. For instance, in the year A.D. 136, Emperor Hadrian completed a wall across the north of England in hope of keeping barbarous tribes behind the barrier. The wall remained until A.D. 383. But by the year 208, Tertullian tells us, there were believers in Jesus Christ on the far side of Hadrian's Wall!

What about that other "Catholic Church"? If you mean the *Roman* Catholic Church, be assured that its claim has no effect on the truth of history. The Church is universal with Jesus Christ as its Head. He left no instructions regarding any local seat of power or earthly substitute—whether at Rome, Constantinople, Canterbury, or elsewhere. The only Church to which the New Testament ascribes authority is sanctified by God to witness throughout the world that Jesus Christ is Lord. This is the Holy Catholic Church which you affirm in the words of the Apostles' Creed.

Unity among Believers

In His prayer in John 17, Jesus specifically called for unity among His followers: "that they may be one." Various organized attempts to insure or recapture unity within the Christian Church were carried on through the early councils at Nicaea, at Constantinople, at Chalcedon, and so on. At the beginning of the 20th century, a renewed call for unity resulted in the development of "the ecumenical movement."

Perhaps no phrase causes quite so diverse reactions among Christians as "ecumenical movement." The word "ecumenical" comes from the Greek word meaning *house*. In other words, the intention of the ecumenical movement is to unify those who call themselves Christians, like a family all under one roof.

Yet to North American fundamentalists, ecumenism is immediately equated with satanic sabotage. In their eyes, the fact that professing Christians from other denominations express their understanding of the Gospel in different terms means that those who differ are in a questionable relationship with God. Indeed, some evangelicals view the ecumenical movement expressed in the World Council of Churches as part of the international Marxist conspiracy.

Others see the ecumenical movement in somewhat less dramatic light. It's a human attempt to improve upon the human failings within the visible Church. As such, the ecumenical movement—like any other human institution—will recreate some of the very ills it seeks to correct.

It's also worth noting that evangelical missionaries from North America—even those from some of the most "separated" fundamentalistic groups—often discover new conditions prevailing overseas. They find a bond of Christian brotherhood with Christians from denominations thought to be suspect at home. One Baptist missionary told me, "In an emergency we find that bandages from a World Council of Churches' shipment work just as well as our own!"

It is far better to remember that we're all a tiny minority in a world desperately needing the healing power of Jesus Christ. We can spend our time fighting with each other over whether or not the other person has dotted every *i* and crossed every *t*. We can pride ourselves on our separateness and denominational purity. Or we can reach out to other professing Christians and become with them part of the human chain that hauls sinking souls out of the quicksand of sin and death to stand on the Rock that is Christ.

His warning, "Not everyone who says to me, 'Lord, Lord,' will enter the kingdom of heaven" (Matt. 7:21), applies with equal force to those who find fellowship in the ecumenical movement and to those who shun it. After all, the true test of who belongs in the universal Church isn't where we place our membership but in whom we put our trust.

9

". . . The Communion of Saints . . ."

My favorite recreation is running. Not jogging, but *running*. To me jogging is for near victims of cardiac arrest; running is for athletes.

Almost every afternoon, I take to the roads for a workout. As I do, I realize I'm risking my safety, if not my life. There's something about the sight of a runner—in my part of the country, at any rate—that brings out the nastiness in large dogs and some people. In recent years, I've been intimidated by countless German shepherds and bitten by a vicious weimaraner. I've also been threatened by a gang of tough youths, had countless cans and glass bottles thrown at me from passing cars, and been steered off the edge of the road by numerous drivers.

But I know from other happy experiences that running isn't so dangerous in other regions. In Seattle, Washington, for instance, Green Lake is a haven for runners of all ages and conditions— men and women, boys and girls—colorfully garbed in fashionable warm-up suits or wearing faded sweatshirts. These people have come to run.

Pairs and groups set out together for their exercise and mutual enjoyment. Individuals may choose, if they wish, the loneliness of the long-distance runner; or they may find companionship merely by asking, "Mind if I tag along?" A nod, a smile, and an instant bond has been formed. Green Lake is a communion of athletes.

A Fellowship

The Church of Jesus Christ is also a communion, a fellowship. The Greek word is *koinōnia,* one of whose meanings is "partnership." We know this meaning in connection with legal contracts involving a business enterprise. It means that two parties have agreed to share both profit and loss in their common interest.

Another word closely related is "community." It derives from a Latin word meaning "mutual participation." We think of various community endeavors to celebrate past historical events or to restore a landmark site, community boosters raising funds for the high school band's uniforms. In all these activities, the welfare of those concerned brings them together in a common drive to achieve as a group what no one member could accomplish alone.

This is the intention behind the Apostles' Creed's "the communion of saints." It is the mutual benefit of each member of the Holy Catholic Church, working, striving, loving, living not for oneself but for the Lord and for each other.

"No man is an island, entire of itself; every man is a piece of the continent, a part of the main," wrote poet-preacher John Donne in "Meditation XVII." In human form, not even the Son of God could endure the loneliness of life without friends and companions. He chose twelve men to accompany Him, three of whom became His intimates. Many more drifted around Him, like hangers-on; but when His teaching became too stringent, they left. " 'Do you want to leave too?' Jesus asked the Twelve. Simon Peter answered Him, 'Lord, to whom shall we go? You have the words of eternal life' " (John 6:67-68).

The Twelve

Who were these first members of the Christian community? What sort of men were they? Luke tells us that they were selected, after much prayer, from the larger following of disciples. "One of those days Jesus went out into the hills to pray, and spent the night praying to God. When morning came, He called His disciples to Him and chose twelve of them, whom he also designated apostles: Simon (whom He named Peter), his brother Andrew, James, John, Philip, Bartholomew, Matthew, Thomas, James son of Alphaeus, Simon who was called the Zealot, Judas son of James, and Judas Iscariot, who became a traitor" (Luke 6:12-16).

These were ordinary men, with the same needs and abilities we possess. What made them different from the rest? We'll never know! But Jesus saw in each of these men a potential leader in the great work He would leave for them to do.

Jesus grouped His followers around Himself. He was the center of their fellowship, the One whom they came to worship as Lord. But from the beginning of His ministry, Jesus Christ appears to have drawn some individuals closer to Himself than others. Or, to put it another way, while the original

Twelve expanded first to 70, then to 120, and on Pentecost to more than 3,000, Jesus chose an inner circle of just three men—Peter, and two brothers, James and John.

Jesus had no "teacher's pets." He didn't show any kind of favoritism. He was harder on Peter than on any other apostle. He specifically rejected the effort of Zebedee's wife to gain preferred status for her sons. Why then did He select three men for the privilege of sharing with Him His glory and His anguish?

One answer may be that Jesus Christ was preparing His Church through men to whom its administration would be entrusted. He had certain lessons to teach, certain tests to be passed, as part of their apprenticeship.

The principle Jesus seems to have been advocating is that of concentric influence. Just as a stone dropped into a pool of water causes ripples from the point of impact outward, so a teacher instructs a few pupils. Those few thereafter teach others, and so the circle of influence widens. Yet all the circles revolve around the same center.

No one belonging to the circle of saints is ever out of communion with that living Center. The most well-known of the Twelve was an impulsive and strong-willed individual. Simon bar-Jona—or if we'd modernize his name—Simon Johnson or Simon Jones—had been his name before he met Jesus of Nazareth. Jesus took a long look at him and probably said, "Your name doesn't fit you. I'm going to call you Cephas—I'm going to call you Petros" (see John 1:42). If Jesus had been speaking French, he'd have named Simon *Pierre*. What was important: Peter's new name suited his new responsibilities. Peter means "rock." Jesus called him *Rocky*!

We'd never have heard of the Apostle Peter, if it hadn't been for his brother Andrew. We know very little about this man: he was a follower of John the Baptist. Thus we can infer that he was devout, earnestly seeking for the Messiah. Presumably, he was a fisherman like his brother. But the most important thing we know about "Andy Jones" is that when he met Jesus of Nazareth, he was so full of joy and excitement, he couldn't keep it to himself. "The first thing Andrew did was to find his brother Simon and tell him, 'We have found the Messiah'" (John 1:41).

Jesus Christ also gave nicknames to James and John, the sons of Zebedee. He called them "Sons of Thunder" (Mark 3:17). What this meant, what prompted their receiving this name, we don't know. But we do know that if they were the cause of occasional reverberations within the band of apostles, they probably inherited their forwardness and lack of tact from their mother, Mrs. Zebedee. Remember her little ploy to gain a favored place for her sons in the coming Kingdom of God? (see Matt. 20:20-28)

This first Christian community demonstrates a great truth about the Church of Jesus Christ: there's ample room for every temperament and personality. Yet there's no room for party politics or narrow opinions in "the communion of saints." Two of Jesus Christ's apostles represented the kind of political opposition we might never expect to mix without explosion. Imagine in our day two Christians in Quebec—one supporting the government of Canada in Ottawa, the other advocating Quebec's separation from the rest of the nation. Or in the United States, two deacons in the same church: one an administrator in the Department of Health, Education and Welfare, charged with overseeing a program of forced busing; the other, a member of the John Birch Society. Would there be any hope of reconciling such opponents?

The gulf between Matthew the publican and Simon the Zealot must have been as great. Matthew was a collaborator with the Roman government, a tax collector who took his share of the taxes and made his living off the oppression of his own people. Simon was a guerilla fighter, a revolutionary committed to the violent overthrow of everything Matthew represented. Yet the community of believers in Jesus Christ had room for both of them.

We could go through the whole list of names and find the Apostles' human qualities developed and their weaknesses overcome by the worship of Jesus Christ and the love His presence developed. Thomas, the doubter, and Judas Iscariot, the betrayer, had known firsthand the reality of this fellowship. When they cut themselves off from it—as Thomas did on the Resurrection Day, as Judas Iscariot did by his treason—they came to know the bitterness of their personal decisions.

But before we come down too hard on Thomas and Judas Iscariot, let's be honest. In our self-righteousness, it's easy to condemn their doubt and disbelief. It's more difficult to recognize our own faces in the group of professed believers who "all deserted Him and fled" (Matt. 26:56). How much worse is it to be a Judas Iscariot than to be one of the deserters? Is there really any difference? How painful it is for us to admit that we have great difficulty standing true instead of following the cowards, the deniers, the false friends.

Thank God the Apostles' Creed goes on to say, "I believe in . . . the forgiveness of sins." How like God the Father, His loving Son, and the gracious Holy Spirit to offer forgiveness and restoration to those who participate in "the communion of saints"!

When Jesus met Simon Peter by the Sea of Tiberias and challenged him with the words, "Do you love Me more than all else?" Jesus addressed him in the same terms as at their first meeting: "Simon, son of John (see John 1:42 and John 21:15-17). Not till the shamed Apostle had exorcised his guilt in three confessions of love for three denials, could he once again be known by his new name, Simon Peter the Rock.

And so, a study of the first Christian community, the Twelve, reveals that one of the marks of "the communion of saints" is its diversity. This seems to be a contradiction in terms: "communion" and "diversity"? But it's really a paradox out of whose tension develops a great truth. For the strength belonging to the Christian community in its vast diversity is the same strength that derives from that community's unity of purpose. In fact, the motto of the United States of America, "*E pluribus unum*," might apply very well to the Church of Jesus Christ: "Out of many, one."

Practical Koinonia

Besides its sense of community, "the communion of saints" has several additional meanings. At its most practical level, *koinōnia* referred to both the sharing of possessions held in common and the contribution to others' needs (see Acts 2:42-47, Rom. 15:26, and Heb. 13:16).

From Luke's account of the Early Church's rapid growth, we can tell that one means of instructing new believers was to keep them in constant association with other believers. While there doesn't appear to have been a hostel in which large groups may have lived, we understand from Luke that "all the believers were together and had everything in common. Selling their possessions and goods, they gave to anyone as he had need. Every day they continued to meet together in the temple courts. They broke bread in their homes and ate together with glad and sincere hearts" (Acts 2:44-46).

The success of this teaching program has certainly been borne out in many comtemporary congregations which have discovered that the way to get a crowd together for some worthy purpose is to sponsor a church supper! But, as the apostles also discovered, such practical matters as how much should be shared can lead to distracting and distressing spiritual problems. The story of Ananias and Sapphira and the complaint of the Greek-speaking Christians illustrate the point (see Acts 4:32—5:12 and 6:1-7).

From the Early Church's example, we can take another most important lesson. To them, there was no division between the sacred and secular. Worship was possible in the most elementary social act: communal eating. We read of their meeting for "the breaking of bread and to pray" (Acts 2:42). We customarily suppose this "breaking of bread" to have been the reenactment of the Lord's Supper, what we also call Holy Communion. But for the earliest followers of Jesus Christ, the sharing of their food at every meal was a consecrated act.

As the ritual of the Early Church became more formalized, with times and seasons set aside and hymns or prayers designated, the observance of the Lord's Supper certainly became distinct from all other eating and drinking (see 1 Cor. 11:18-34). Yet it was in the multiplying of bread and fish that many believed in Jesus of Nazareth (see John 6:1-14); it was in "the breaking of the bread" that the two companions at Emmaus recognized the risen Lord (see Luke 24:28-35). It was in His eating with them that His apostles confirmed Jesus' physical resurrection (see John 22:13).

One of the earliest recorded prayers is the eucharistic blessing, *Maranatha,* an Aramaic expression. Some of our English Bibles translate it "Come, O Lord" (1 Cor. 16:22). It's surely an eschatological prayer of yearning for the return of Jesus Christ. But Oscar Cullmann, in his book *Early Christian Worship,* suggests that the prayer's primary office may have been to call forth the blessing of the Lord's presence at table: "Come, O Lord, to this table as You did in the upper room and at Emmaus."

What joy for a Christian family to sit together around the dining room table and, in giving thanks for the provision of food, ask for and receive assurance of the Lord's presence! So we may participate, in one of our most necessary daily acts, in "the communion of saints."

> Be present at our table, Lord;
> Be here and everywhere adored.
> These mercies bless and grant that we
> May feast in Paradise with Thee.

If our thanksgiving before meals is to mean anything, it must be translated into sharing with those who would otherwise be without food and shelter. The Church should always set an example to secular government of what it means to be concerned for the general welfare. At a time when many municipalities, states, and whole nations are over-burdened by masses of poverty-stricken people, Christians can't become smug and uncaring about those in need. If for no one else, the Church is at least responsible for the poverty-stricken among God's people. But can our giving stop there? To the stingy Corinthians, Paul wrote, "Remember this: Whoever sows sparingly will also reap sparingly, and whoever sows generously will also reap generously. Each man should give what he has decided in his heart to give, not reluctantly or under compulsion, for God loves a cheerful giver" (2 Cor. 9:6-7). And Jesus commended generosity in the Sermon on the Mount: "Give, and it will be given to you. A good measure, pressed down, shaken together, and running over, will be poured into your lap. For with the measure you use, it will be measured to you" (Luke 6:38).

The Koinonia of Suffering

Another aspect of "the communion of saints" extends to sharing the physical suffering of our brothers and sisters who suffer for the sake of Christ. The Christian is promised hardship in a world hostile to Jesus Christ (see John 16:33). Most of us in North America live year after year without a challenge to our right to worship, without having to risk our lives for what we believe. Perhaps this privilege lulls us into thinking that the

Bible is overly dramatic when it speaks of persecution. Throughout the world many Christians can verify the Bible's truth by the bruises and scars on their bodies.

We ought to be prepared to enter, with Paul, into the *koinōnia* of Christ's sufferings (see Phil. 3:10). We also ought to be aware that we may be called upon to suffer alone. Certainly Jesus Christ Himself suffered without the solace of faithful friends. Paul too writes of having been abandoned (see 2 Tim. 4:9-10). This may well be the cost of discipleship.

The Witnesses

Finally, "the communion of saints" means that the testimony of the ages continues unbroken through all time. Believers who have preceded us along the Glory Way are our forerunners, that great "cloud of witnesses" (Heb. 12:1), whose example of faith we emulate. By studying their lives and service, we share their triumphs and losses—and their ultimate vindication.

Here is no call for pagan idolatry or veneration of canonized saints. Rather, it's a clear recognition of the Bible's principle, that succeeding generations learn from their elders the traditions and expectations of the Gospel.

The Body of Christ, knit together by His redeeming love, can never be severed, not even by death. Between those already enjoying the heavenly sphere and those of us who still await its attainment, communion may be known. Their Hallelujah Chorus rings in our souls, if we will only listen for the encouragement and urging onward from those who died in faith believing.

"Blessed are the dead who die in the Lord from now on, . . . They will rest from their labor, for their deeds will follow them" (Rev. 14:13). Those deeds become our example of grace and the Spirit's seal upon their continuing communion with us.

10

" . . . The Forgiveness of Sins . . ."

The case of Gary Gilmore, a Utah prisoner convicted of murder and condemned to die before a firing squad, considerably disturbed American society. Gilmore was to be the first person executed in over nine years because the Supreme Court had overturned death penalty laws. Those opposing new capital punishment laws sought to stay his execution.

Unlike the usual prisoner, this condemned man didn't seek to avoid his sentence. He claimed his right to have the court's judgment upon him fulfilled. "I have accepted the court's decision," he told a hearing, "and I want to die in dignity like a man. I don't want sympathy and I don't want forgiveness."

Gilmore's case fascinated us because we don't expect to find people who openly admit wrongdoing and who also demand to be permitted to pay the penalty—especially when that penalty is death. Psychiatrists explained the bizarre Gilmore case as an instance of "death wish," self-hatred so unremitting as to be suicidal. Or was his simply such an abiding sense of guilt that he felt beyond the reach of forgiveness? Christians can only lament that any man should feel so desperately alienated, especially from God, that he would refuse all offers of mercy.

Of course, Gilmore, like every human being, could have appropriated the Gospel of Jesus Christ. For acceptance of the Good News brings "the forgiveness of sins."

In some degree, a consciousness of sin grips us all. What to do about it is man's major problem. Religion tries to provide means of atoning for sin— by animal sacrifice, by flagellation, by self-denial, by charitable gifts, by good works. But these are never enough. Failure to satisfy religion's standards condemns man as much as if he'd made no attempt to be religious.

The Offer of Forgiveness
The Gospel declares our efforts to be unavailing, however noble their intentions. Instead, the Gospel announces that the only hope we have is through God's way of righting wrong. (see Rom. 1:17 and 3:22). His way has nothing to do with any attempt by us to pay the penalty for our own sins. God's way leads us to believe in His sovereignty, in His desire to forgive us, and in His power to give us new life through the death, resurrection, and exaltation of Jesus Christ.

But while God is "the Father Almighty, Maker of heaven and earth," He does not force forgiveness on us. He has created in us a free will, the power to accept or reject forgiveness. We can, if we choose, turn away from God's grace. We can ignore what He offers. We can insist on going our own way. "There is a way that seemeth right unto a man," says the proverb, "but the end thereof are the ways of death" (Prov. 16:25). To everyone, God offers the same clear choice expressed by Moses to the Israelites: "I have set before you life and death, blessing and cursing: therefore choose life, that both thou and thy seed may live" (Deut. 30:19). Forgiveness is offered. The pardon has been signed and sealed. Nothing remains except for us to forsake our cell on death row and make our way into the glorious freedom of new life. This is the Gospel's unique message of forgiveness for our sins.

The gods of world religions are often depicted as vicious, cruel, bloodthirsty, vengeful, and implacable. Forgiveness is unknown to their worshipers. The most they can hope for is to appease the gods. But the Bible teaches that forgiveness is a characteristic of God the Father. It is made possible by the sacrifice of God the Son, and is guaranteed by the gifts of God the Holy Spirit. The prophet Micah described the differences between the God of Israel and pagan deities: "Who is a God like unto Thee, that pardoneth iniquity, and passeth by the transgression of the remnant of His heritage? He retaineth not His anger forever, because He delighteth in mercy. He will turn again, He will have compassion upon us; He will subdue our iniquities; and Thou wilt cast all their sins into the depths of the sea" (Micah 7:18-19).

The poet-king sang, "Bless the Lord, O my soul, and forget not all His benefits: who forgiveth all thine iniquities; who healeth all thy diseases" (Ps. 103:2-3). Our God prefers forgiveness to condemnation. But we can't take His mercy for granted.

He is the God of justice and requires that the sinner repent before he can be forgiven.

Repentance

What does it mean to *repent*? We could consult Webster's, but the Bible gives an excellent description of repentance in the word of the Lord to King Solomon: "If My people, which are called by My name, shall humble themselves, and pray, and seek My face, and turn from their wicked ways: then will I hear from heaven, and will forgive their sin, and will heal their land" (2 Chron. 7:14). This verse presents simple-to-understand conditions for forgiveness and pardon: submit, pray, seek God, turn away from evil. Begin by bowing in submission and humility before God, acknowledging His sovereignty and our complete dependence upon Him. Of course, this hurdle will block a proud person from obtaining forgiveness. Prayer, seeking God, finding from Him the grace to resist evil and turn away from its allurements are all easier than the initial yielding of our pride and submitting to His authority.

When former President Gerald Ford issued a blanket pardon to Richard Nixon, both men showed a fundamental misunderstanding of law and grace. The resigned president had never been formally accused or indicted, tried or convicted of any crime. According to law, he was ineligible for a pardon, having been convicted of nothing from which to be pardoned. But in offering a pardon under these circumstances, President Ford implied Nixon's guilt of unspecified crimes. In accepting the pardon without a word of repentance, Nixon convicted himself in the minds of many Americans.

Had the disgraced former president admitted his wrongdoing, he might have found forgiveness from the nation.

Of course, God alone is the Judge of men. He doesn't require anything more of us than that we cease our arrogant separation from Him. "Let the wicked forsake his way," says Isaiah, "and the unrighteous man his thoughts: and let him return unto the Lord, and He will have mercy upon him; and to our God, for He will abundantly pardon" (Isa. 55:7).

External Evidence

In Luke 5:17-26, we find one of the most dramatic stories in the ministry of Jesus. A paralyzed man has been carried on a stretcher by his friends to the house where Jesus is teaching. But when they arrive, they find the house full of ardent listeners. There's no way to get their friend before the teacher from Nazareth. Not to be deterred, they take him up the stairs outside the house to the skylight in the roof. After removing enough tiles, they lower the stretcher into the middle of the crowd and thus gain Jesus' attention.

The text informs us that the faith of the paralytic's friends moved Jesus. But He didn't respond as they'd expected; He didn't immediately heal their stricken friend. Instead, He said, "Friend, your sins are forgiven" (Luke 5:20).

Jesus' antagonists in the crowd were outraged. At once they began to discuss His apparent blasphemy. In doing so, they played straight into Jesus' hands. They asked the very question He needed to have asked: "Who can forgive sins but God alone?" (Luke 5:21).

At this moment, Jesus faced them with the most searing logic. He gave them two humanly impossible options: Which is easier, He asked, to forgive a man's sins or to heal his paralysis? The answer —unspoken by His stunned critics—was obvious enough: Neither act is easy, both require the power of God; whoever could do one undoubtedly possessed the power to perform the other.

The external evidence of forgiven sins isn't always readily demonstrable while the healing of a paralytic, on the other hand, is clearly manifest. In this rare instance, therefore, Jesus chose to demonstrate that, indeed, He had power both to forgive sins and to heal the body.

The healing was almost incidental to the forgiveness. It was merely the visible sign of the invisible but greater deliverance the man had been granted. Jesus is always more concerned about deliverance from sin than He is about physical relief. While He healed some, He came to forgive us all.

The prodigal son (Luke 15:17-20) was no fool. He knew the difference between a mansion and a pigsty, between a banquet and a swill pail. It may have been that he was utterly sincere in returning home; or he might have been less than sincere, merely willing to eat crow for the sake of a full stomach and a comfortable bed. Both his rehearsed speech and his elder brother's suspicion that he was taking their father for a ride ought to cause us at least to reserve judgment momentarily.

A moment is all that's needed, however, because the father took charge of things instantly. He saw the young man coming while he was still a dim figure on the horizon. But that gait, that shuffle, was unmistakable to the eyes that had yearned for some sight of him! The old man gathered up his robe and, according to Kenneth E. Bailey in *The Cross and the Prodigal,* humiliated himself, discarding his dignity by running to meet his younger son.

Now the prodigal son began his speech. The words were just as he'd rehearsed them, first in the pigpen, then along the way: "Father, I have sinned against heaven and against you. I am no longer worthy to be called your son" (Luke 15:21).

Just as the son was about to go on with the rest of his speech—the part about being willing to make a deal with his father, to work like a common slave to pay back the wasted inheritance—his father interrupted. He had heard all he needed to hear. "Father" acknowledges the station each man holds. It reestablishes the son's submission to his father. "I have sinned" admitted the truth of his wrongdoing; "I am no longer worthy" indicated a plea for forgiveness.

Whether or not the son had intended to connive his way home made no difference. The father offered forgiveness in abundance. The erring son claimed it gladly.

The father of the parable corresponds to our heavenly Father, whose characteristic forgiveness we've already attested. But while the prodigal's actions are important, the Father also wants to hear words of repentance. We've all experienced the unpleasantness of a difficult reconciliation. Sometimes an offender would rather present us with a box of candy or a dozen red roses than say, "I'm sorry. I was wrong. Please forgive me." The candy, the roses, are a gesture, but we're looking for more. We need to hear the words that will cleanse the wound and make healing possible—

words that will elicit from us spontaneous forgiveness.

So, for us to receive the Father's full pardon, we must first end our rebellion, submit to His authority, and return from our sinful ways. Then, as in the Episcopal Prayer of General Confession, we must say and mean with all our hearts words such as these:

> Almighty God, Father of our Lord Jesus Christ, Maker of all things, Judge of all men: We acknowledge and bewail our manifold sins and wickedness, which we, from time to time, most grievously have committed, by thought, word, and deed, against Thy Divine Majesty, provoking most justly Thy wrath and indignation against us. We do earnestly repent, and are heartily sorry for these our misdoings; the remembrance of them is grievous unto us; the burden of them is intolerable. Have mercy upon us, have mercy upon us, most merciful Father; for Thy Son our Lord Jesus Christ's sake, forgive us all that is past; and grant that we may ever hereafter serve and please Thee in newness of life, to the honor and glory of Thy Name; through Jesus Christ our Lord. Amen.

From the Apostle John we have assurance that such a prayer will be received. "If we confess our sins, He is faithful and just and will forgive us our sins and purify us from all unrighteousness (1 John 1:9).

Principles of Forgiveness

To affirm belief in "the forgiveness of sins" means that we accept the Good News of the Gospel. In Jesus Christ, "we have redemption through His blood, the forgiveness of sins" (Eph. 1:7; see also Col. 1:14). But this promise of forgiveness isn't reserved only for the relationship between God and me; it must also extend to my dealings with other human beings whom God also forgives. The great clause in the prayer Jesus Christ taught His disciples reminds us to pray, "Forgive us our debts, as we also have forgiven our debtors" (Matt. 6:12). Or as another version states, "Forgive us the wrong we have done, as we have forgiven those who have wronged us" (NEB). The tense of the verbs in the petition suggests "Forgive us *now* as we have *already* forgiven." This is the standard principle of Christian forgiveness (see Matt. 5:23-24). Surely this is also the corollary to "the Golden Rule" (see Matt. 7:12), to the principle of "measure for measure" (see Matt. 7:1-2; Luke 6:37-38). We can't expect forgiveness if we withhold forgiveness.

Another principle is the need for reparation to those whom we have wronged. In the Law of Moses, full reparation plus one-fifth in penalty was the demand (see Num. 5:5-7). In the New Testament, the example of Zaccheus challenges us with our obligation (see Luke 19:1-10). After the diminutive publican met Jesus of Nazareth and felt convicted of his fraudulence, he promised to give back half of his ill-gotten wealth to charities and offered to pay 400% damages to anyone he had wronged.

The forgiveness we receive from God cancels our debt to Him. But if, by our sin, we have injured our brother, we're responsible to pay our share of his injury.

Perhaps no single statement in all the Bible so beautifully sums up the teaching and method of Christian forgiveness as this: "Be kind and compassionate to one another, forgiving each other, just as in Christ God forgave you" (Eph. 4:32). All the conditions are here set forth—theological, moral, ethical, and personal.

Theologically, our forgiveness by God the Father is provided through Jesus Christ, with the Holy Spirit's presence in our lives as proof. Having therefore accepted this forgiveness ourselves, we're morally obligated to the reciprocal relationship God ordains—forgiving each other as He has forgiven us. The ethics of forgiveness will be shown in kindness and compassion, in an absence of haughtiness, in the common understanding of our mutual human frailty. And since no one is exempt from God's grace, our personal dealings with every human being must be in terms of Christian forgiveness.

In Jesus Christ we have the most arresting example possible. At the moment of His greatest anguish, He called out, "Father, forgive them for they do not know what they are doing" (Luke 23:34). In the face of such an example, how can we fail to pray with the hymnwriter Hans Leo Hassler:

> What language shall I borrow to thank Thee, dearest Friend,
> For this, Thy dying sorrow, Thy pity without end?
> O make me Thine forever; and should I fainting be,
> Lord, let me never, never outlive my love to Thee.

11

" . . . *The Resurrection of the Body* . . ."

One of the most famous moments in drama is the scene in Shakespeare's *Hamlet* in which the Prince of Denmark examines the skull of the court jester, his boyhood entertainer, Yorick. As the gravedigger tells Hamlet whose remains he holds in his hand, Hamlet at first feels revulsion. Then he begins to speculate on the state of being dead. He asks his companion Horatio if even Alexander the Great looked like this—and smelled so! Then Hamlet exclaims, "To what base uses we may return, Horatio!" Hamlet reasons that the noble body of Alexander the Great, rotting like anyone else's, will decay into loam, from which might be made a plug to stop a beer barrel!

Death in the Midst of Life
This scene affects every audience because no fact about our mortality is less acceptable to us than this: our bodies are corruptible. Within hours after the breath of life leaves us, we begin to pass into the earliest stages of decomposition. Yet our rotting away doesn't begin with the onslaught of rigor

mortis. As the burial service says, "In the midst of life we are in death." No matter how carefully we guard our health, each breath we draw brings us closer to the grave. And when we have died, no matter how skilled the embalmer may be, morticians' cosmetics can do nothing to take away the pallor of death. No matter how expensive the coffin, it can do little to delay the decay that turns flesh into dust.

Surely the psalmist understood this when he wrote: "Behold, Thou hast made my days as an handbreadth; and mine age is as nothing before Thee: verily every man at his best state is altogether vanity. Surely every man walketh in a vain show" (Ps. 39:5-6).

Plastic surgery and dentures, toupees and transplants can't preserve us from the inevitable breakdown and collapse of our mortal bodies. No matter how elegantly we adorn ourselves with clothing and jewels, we are still essentially attempting to disguise the fact of our impending demise. This is what the psalmist means by his statement, that "every man at his best state is altogether *vanity*"— empty, foolish, ineffectual. No wonder that, in the same psalm, he uses the metaphor of a moth-eaten garment to describe our physical decay.

Modern secularism's chief concern is to combat death by whatever delaying tactics possible. Even after death, the process of cryogenics carries on the struggle—by freezing the corpse until a cure for the disease that killed can be invented and its serum injected, hopefully to bring the body back to life. So far, however, success at this technique has been limited entirely to pipedreaming!

As an alternative to overcoming death, "the cult

of youth" dominates our culture. Language, commerce and politics, fashions and entertainment, health and appetites are all subordinated to modern "youthomania." Not long ago, people expected to "grow old gracefully." Today we call our elderly "senior citizens," often putting them in nursing homes so as not to remind us of the natural fact of aging. We retire men from business at age 60 and expect them to find purpose and meaning in life at the end of a shuffleboard stick. We glamorize inexperience and give to youth the work belonging to adults. We turn middle-aged women into ludicrously painted and clothed young girls in a futile quest for youthfulness. Men carefully use hair coloring to bring back a youthful appearance.

No wonder some Christians, in revolt against the secular idolatry of the body, have adopted an opposite attitude. According to this view, the body is nothing, not "the real me," only "the shell in which I live."

Like all extreme reactions to one abomination, this swings dangerously close to another. True, secular obessions are the "vain show" the psalmist spoke of. Yet to discredit the body is an affront against the Creator who formed man from the dust of the ground, shaped him, and into that shape—that human form—breathed His own divine life. This, too, God called *good*, and sent His Holy Spirit to inhabit the bodies of men and women.

Christianity has always opposed any heresies that devalue the human body. Gnosticism was perhaps the earliest, Manichaeism a later development, establishing a duality between matter and spirit. These heresies disallowed any possibility of goodness in matter. Therefore, Jesus of Nazareth, as a Man in human flesh, could not be the Son of God (see 2 John 7). Modern cults continue to perpetrate the denial that the Son of God would ever deign to appear in human form. These cults thereby make mockery of the claims of Jesus of Nazareth to be the one and only Son. Among modern heresies, Christian Science is most explicit in denying Jesus His place as the Incarnate Son of God.

The Importance of the Resurrection

We've already seen how important the Incarnation is to the Gospel. Without its truth, Jesus would have been just another in a long line of martyrs. We would still have to wait for the One whom His life and sacrifice foreshadow. Similarly, the Resurrection and exaltation would be in the class of famous myths from which the whole world obtains a moral lesson but which nobody treats as historical reality. But to the Christian the Resurrection means that death's stranglehold upon humanity has been broken; the mortal body has achieved immortality. By His exaltation, the Lord Jesus Christ ushers in a new element to the economy of heaven. He paves the way into the presence of God who is spirit, so that other bodies—our bodies—glorified like His, may one day inhabit the sublimity of God.

This is the importance of "the resurrection of the body": It completes God's program to restore us to Himself, made in His image and likeness, made like His dear Son.

Yet the corruption and decay of our flesh is also important, for it fulfills God's awful warning to Adam: "Of every tree of the garden thou mayest freely eat: But of the tree of the knowledge of good and evil, thou shalt not eat of it: for in the day that thou eatest thereof thou shalt surely die (Gen. 2:16-17). That death commenced with the loss of innocence and the onset of aging. Its summons is clear in the dire judgment of God upon Adam, "For dust thou art, and unto dust shalt thou return" (Gen. 3:19). Corruption is also evidence of Satan's original lie, "You shall not surely die" (Gen. 3:4).

The body is precious to God, and its resurrection is God's counter-fulfillment of a plan whereby He might redeem what had been lost in Eden. Perhaps the oldest writing in the Bible is the Book of Job. Its characters date from the time of the patriarchs. Job sat in his wretchedness, refusing to curse God and die. He held out this joyous hope: "For I know that my Redeemer liveth, and that He shall stand at the latter day upon the earth: and though after my skin worms destroy this body, yet in my flesh shall I see God: whom I shall see for myself, and mine eyes shall behold, and not another; though my reins be consumed within me" (Job 19:25-27).

Clearly, Job knew from some source about the coming resurrection of the body. So too, the prophet Isaiah, who saw the restoration of the glory of Israel as a resurrection of God's people from the dead: "Thy dead men shall live, together with my dead body shall they arise. Awake and sing, ye that dwell in dust: for thy dew is as the dew of herbs, and the earth shall cast out the dead" (Isa. 26:19).

This is the tradition of Jewish prophecy in which Saul of Tarsus, schooled as a Pharisee, had been taught. It wasn't difficult for him, once he became Paul an apostle, to recognize in the experience of Jesus Christ what awaits us. Paul spells it out most definitively in 1 Corinthians 15. In verses 1-11, Paul reminds his readers of the historical facts and his authority for imparting them. In verses 12-19, he takes the negative side in the debate, showing the state of things if Christ were not alive. In verses 20-34, with a parenthetic statement or two, he argues positively for the effects of the Resurrection.

A Case for Our Resurrection

Then we come to Paul's case for our resurrection. As he does so often, Paul chooses to reason by analogy. He first uses an agricultural example, then expands the analogy to consider species in nature and classes of stars. "But someone may ask, 'How are the dead raised? With what kind of body will they come?' How foolish! What you sow does not come to life unless it dies. When you sow, you do not plant the body that will be, but just a seed, perhaps of wheat or of something else. But God gives it a body as He has determined, and to each kind of seed He gives its own body" (1 Cor. 15:35-38).

Paul's point is the distinction between what is planted and what is harvested. An acorn doesn't germinate and grow into a larger acorn, but becomes an oak. Yet even the greatest oak, though different in *form* from its seed, carries with it the *substance* of the acorn. The same principle is true of the lights of earth and heaven—different in *type* yet the same in *essence* (see 1 Cor. 15:40-41).

"So it will be with the resurrection of the dead," continues Paul. "The body that is sown is perishable, it is raised imperishable; it is sown in dishonor, it is raised in glory; it is sown in weakness, it is raised in power; it is sown a natural body, it is raised a spiritual body" (1 Cor. 15:42-44).

The analogy is complete: *seed* is to *body* as *harvest* is to *resurrection*. Just as the farmer plants seed in expectation of the harvest, so we bury the body of a believer, awaiting the resurrection harvest. But there's more to this comparison. The farmer looks for something to harvest different from what he planted. Yet it is of the same essence. So we also must look for something different at the Final Harvest. Paul calls it a *mystery*.

The Greek word for "mystery" suggests not so much a complex and insoluble puzzle; that's an *enigma*. Rather, a *mystery* is a secret to be shared only among the inner circle. Paul has a secret to share with us: *There's gonna be some changes made!* Miraculously, the body will die and will be changed. We'll be the same person but not the same body! Age and infirmity will have vanished; bent limbs, broken noses, crossed eyes, damaged eardrums, lungs polluted by emphysema, livers and breasts and stomachs and throats ravaged by cancer—these will all be transformed! And for those of us still physically alive when Jesus Christ returns, the same miracle will occur. Let Paul tell it his way:

> Listen, I tell you a mystery: We shall not all sleep, but we shall all be changed—in a flash, in the twinkling of an eye, at the last trumpet. For the trumpet will sound, the dead will be raised imperishable, and we shall be changed. For the perishable must clothe itself with the imperishable, and the mortal with immortality. When the perishable has been clothed with the imperishable, and the mortal with immortality, then the saying that is written will come true: "Death has been swallowed up in victory."

Where, O death, is your victory?
Where O death, is your sting?
The sting of death is sin, and the power of sin
is the law. But thanks be to God! He gives us
the victory through our Lord Jesus Christ
(1 Cor. 15:51-57).

Try to imagine what Paul is describing. In an
instant of time, from every cemetery and cremato-
rium, from every ocean, lake, and river, from every
continent, rises the glorified host! Bodies once dead
or "in the midst of life . . . in death" quickened by
new life!

In November 1973, my family and I stood on a
windswept hillside in the Hudson River Valley and
lowered my father's body into the ground. His soul,
I know, is present with the Lord. But the anguish
of separating body from soul was suddenly real for
me as the trademark of what death means. Yet on
that day when the trumpet sounds, when the voice
of God speaks, the body of the man I knew as Dad
—Ernest Arthur Lockerbie—will arise to sleep no
more, forever reunited in soul and body. Will I
know him? Of course. Haven't I always known him?

This joyful hope is ours because of the Lord Jesus
Christ, who "by the power that enables Him to
bring everything under His control, will transform
our lowly bodies so that they will be like His
glorious body" (Phil. 3:21).

"The resurrection of the body" completes God's
work of grace. He created us; He redeemed us. At
our resurrection, He restores us to Himself in all
the splendor He intended us to share from the beginning. Once more, He'll look at His handiwork
and declare it "very good."

Then comes "the Life everlasting."

12

". . . And the Life Everlasting. Amen."

Of all the promises in the Bible, none has more to offer than this: "God so loved the world, that He gave His only begotten Son, that whosoever believeth in Him should not perish, but have everlasting life" (John 3:16, KJV). "The life everlasting" is ours as a gift from God, if we *believe*. But while the Creed's concluding phrase points beyond the resurrection of the body and the consummation of history in timeless eternity, the words can and must be read for the present as well. We can possess "the life everlasting" *now,* as the Apostle John explains: "This we proclaim concerning the Word of life. The life appeared; we have seen it and testify to it, and we proclaim to you the eternal life, which was with the Father and has appeared to us. We proclaim to you what we have seen and heard, so that you also may have fellowship with us. And our fellowship is with the Father and with His Son, Jesus Christ" (1 John 1:1-3).

He is the Word of Life, the Water of Life, the Bread of Life, the Resurrection and the Life, the Way, the Truth, and the Life. Indeed, *life* is the theme of the Gospel. It's the Good News that Jesus has come "that they may have life, and have it to the full" (John 10:10). From Adam, every man at birth inherited death. From Jesus Christ, a man can have a new birth into life, not only now but throughout the aeons of eternity. To know "life everlasting" in the ages to come, we must begin living it today.

Views on Life after Death

In directing our thoughts to the future, we need to say more about the word *life*. Some philosophers and religious spokesmen are willing to allow a kind of afterlife, but it's often inferior to the reality we experience now. They talk about some nebulous state of consciousness in a limbo of memory or lingering influence. Bertrand Russell, for instance, claimed that our memory of someone is "the most essential thing in the continuity of a person." The Reformed Jewish litany for the dead declares: "They still live on in our memory of their good deeds." This is why many men and women strive to leave behind them some monument, some work of art, some testimonial to the fact that they once passed this way.

The Bible, however, is starkly clear in affirming its view of "everlasting life." Throughout Scripture, persons live after death, recognizable to each other, animated by eternal vitality, wholly conscious of their environment and of the choice that placed them there. One of Jesus Christ's most fully developed parables is the story of Lazarus and the rich man (see Luke 16:19-31). No story deals more specifically with the realities of life after death. Again, Jesus' description of the final state of those who enter the kingdom, as against those who are cast into outer darkness, leaves no doubt of the contrasting lives to be lived throughout eternity (see Matt. 25:14-46).

What then, is "the life everlasting"? Where do we spend eternity?

Whatever Huckleberry Finn knew about heaven and hell, he learned from Miss Watson, an unlikely teacher. "She said all a body would have to do there was to go around all day with a harp and sing," says Huck Finn of Miss Watson's heaven. He had more sense than to accept that definition of bliss. Having made up his mind not to try for heaven, he "asked her if she reckoned Tom Sawyer would go there, and she said, not by a considerable sight. I was glad about that, because I wanted him and me to be together."

"Heaven for climate, hell for company," says James M. Barrie, giving a quip's support to the view that too much of a good thing can only be dull. It's not amusing, however, to realize that many people who think at all about the afterlife seem to be as ignorant as Huckleberry Finn. Heaven, to them, is the Pearly Gates Country Club, whose membership secretary is St. Peter. Once admitted, we have round after round of enjoyment with angels as our servants. God is the elderly gent we meet back at the celestial clubhouse.

And if there's an opposite place, men jokingly talk about the fellow dressed in something looking like red tights borrowed from last year's Halloween party. And if there's anything painful in the experience, it's only a little jabbing from his majesty's pitchfork!

How different are the views of everlasting life

from the vantage of skepticism and disbelief!
"Parting is all we know of heaven, and all we need
of hell," wrote Emily Dickinson. Henry David
Thoreau defined heaven as "the place which men
avoid." To Jean-Paul Sartre, hell is "other people."
And John Milton's Satan, in *Paradise Lost,* expresses the rebellion of all God's antagonists when
he rages, "Better to reign in hell than serve in
heaven."

Understanding Life Everlasting

Service is perhaps a key to understanding "the life
everlasting." It's meant to be a grand oratorio con-
cert sung by choirs from every nation and tongue,
singing "Hallelujah!" and "Worthy is the Lamb" to
the Messiah Himself. It's meant to be the Father's
welcome-home party for long-lost children. Most of
all, heaven's everlasting life is intended to be a
marriage ceremony, a wedding reception, and an
eternal honeymoon—the perfect union of Jesus
and His Church, the Bridegroom and the Bride.

Throughout immeasurable reaches of eternity the
angels will murmur their wonder at the Bride's
beauty, at the Bridegroom's courage in rescuing her
from the Dragon, at the Father's delight, at the
Spirit's tender care of the Bride during her long
separation from the Bridegroom. And all this time
the choir of cherubim will be lauding the Wedding
Party with "Blessing, and honor, and glory, and
power, be unto Him that sitteth upon the throne,
and unto the Lamb forever and ever" (Rev. 5:13,
KJV). Meanwhile the orchestra of seraphim will be
playing variations on a theme of "Holy, Holy,
Holy." It will be the fulfillment of the ideal celebration every festival ever aspired to be!

And that's just the point! Satan and his cynical stooges hate beauty and joy and celebration. He despises service as a sign of weakness. He's contemptuous of praise as flattery. His jealousy of the Son as the Apple of the Father's eye has made him ravenous to seduce the Bride and win her for himself. Like Eris in the Greek myth, he would incite discord wherever he could, even in heaven, if possible. But he's exiled to hell, where he lords it over his minions in imitation of the power he once tried to usurp.

The Mystery of Life Everlasting

No one knows exactly, of course, what heaven is or how "the life everlasting" is to be lived. Even the Apostle John's great vision is represented to us in terms we recognize as symbolic of something else. But that's all as it should be. The joys we treasure most are usually veiled from us until just the right moment—like a bride never seen in her bridal gown by her husband until she approaches him at the altar.

That's why our imagination has been given to us—to carry us beyond the limits of the little we know about eternal life, to stand in awe before the sealed door and wonder what lies on the other side. Of this we can be sure: All the saints and seers agree that "the life everlasting" is the start of something big!

"In my end is my beginning," wrote the poet T. S. Eliot; and in another poem he said,

> We shall not cease from exploration
> And the end of all our exploring
> Will be to arrive where we started
> And know the place for the first time.

Another Christian writer, C. S. Lewis, concluded his Chronicles of Narnia with *The Last Battle*. At the end the children once again meet Aslan the Lion, who tells them that because of a railway accident, they have left "the Shadowlands," having been numbered among the dead. Then Aslan speaks in comforting terms school children could best appreciate: "The term is over: the holidays have begun. The dream is ended: this is the morning." With the great gift of simplicity with which God blessed him, Lewis touched upon the most compelling reason for our spiritual homesickness—our yearning to be at home with the Father forever. He finished his children's story with this rapturous truth:

> And as Aslan spoke, he no longer looked to them like a lion; but the things that began to happen after that were so great and beautiful that I cannot write them. And for us this is the end of all the stories, and we can most truly say that they all lived happily ever after. But for them it was only the beginning of the real story. All their life in this world and all their adventures in Narnia had only been the cover and the title page: now at last they were beginning Chapter One of the Great Story which no one on earth has read: which goes on for ever: in which every chapter is better than the one before.[1]

The Final Word

Amen is a word we hear so often that it sometimes

---

[1] C. S. Lewis, *The Last Battle* (New York: Macmillan Publishing Company, 1956), p. 165.

doesn't even register on our consciousness. At the end of most prayers, at the end of solemn hymns, as a choral benediction, as an encouragement to the preacher from someone in the pews, as a response in worship: it's one of the most common words in our church experience. Here we find it again, like a caboose at the end of a long train, bringing up the rear of the Apostles' Creed.

Amen means three things. As "truly" or "certainly," it affirms what has gone before. In the case of the Creed, *amen* gives the stamp of veracity to the claims therein, declaring in effect, "These words are true."

As "so let it be" or "so be it," the word assents to every doctrine taught in the Creed, confirms them by ratifying with *amen.* Like the signature of the president on a law passed by both Houses of Congress, *amen* sets its seal of approval.

Lastly, *amen* is one of the names by which the Lord Jesus Christ identified Himself. He is the Word, the final Word; in John's apocalyptic vision, the Lord introduces Himself as "the Amen, the faithful and true witness, the Ruler of God's creation" (Rev. 3:14).

We dare not say or sing this word glibly. To utter "amen" is to transcend the mere sound patterns of speech and the definitions of meaning. To utter "amen" is to place ourselves within the very sanctuary of God, confronting His holiness and righteousness, His justice and truth, and declaring our willingness to stand fast for what we believe.

John Calvin, in his *Institutes,* wrote concerning the Apostles' Creed, "We consider to be beyond controversy the only point that ought to concern us: that the whole history of our faith is summed up in it succinctly and in definite order, and that it contains nothing that is not vouchsafed by genuine testimonies of Scripture."

Can you say, "I believe . . ."? Can you also say, "Amen"?

Suggested Reading

Baillie, D. M. *God Was in Christ*. New York: Charles Scribner's Sons, 1948.

Baillie, John. *Our Knowledge of God*. London: Oxford University Press, 1939.

Bruce, F. F. *Tradition, Old and New*. Grand Rapids: Zondervan Publishing House, 1971.

Cullmann, Oscar. *Early Christian Worship*. Naperville, Ill.: Alec R. Allenson, Inc., 1953.

Delling, D. Gerhard. *Worship in the New Testament*. London: Darton, Longman & Todd, 1962.

Denney, James. *The Death of Christ*. London: Hodder and Stoughton, 1905.

Douglas, J. D., ed. *The New International Dictionary of the Christian Church*. Grand Rapids: Zondervan Publishing House, 1974.

Henry, Carl F. H., ed. *Basic Christian Doctrines*. New York: Holt, Rinehart & Winston, 1962.

Kelly, J. N. D. *Early Christian Creeds*. New York: David Mckay Company, Inc., 1972.

Lewis, C. S. *Miracles*. New York: Macmillan Publishing Company, Inc., 1963.

Lockerbie, D. Bruce. *The Liberating Word: Art and the Mystery of the Gospel*. Grand Rapids: Eerdmans Publishing Company, 1974.

_____. *The Cosmic Center*. Grand Rapids: Eerdmans Publishing Company, 1977.

Martin, Ralph P. *Worship in the Early Church*. Revised edition. Grand Rapids: Eerdmans Publishing Company, 1975.

Runia, Klaas. *I Believe in God*. London: Tyndale Press, 1963.

Walsh, Chad, et al. *The Apostles' Creed: An Introduction*. Cincinnati: Forward Movement Publications, 1966.

Whale, J. S. *Christian Doctrine*. New York: Cambridge University Press, 1941.

Whitaker, E. C. *Documents of the Baptismal Liturgy*. Naperville, Ill.: Alec R. Allenson, Inc., 1970.